W9-ALV-785

The Taming

of the Shrew

CORINNE J. NADEN
INTRODUCTION BY JOSEPH SOBRAN

mc **Marshall Cavendish**
Benchmark
New York

Special thanks to Kim Noling, professor of English at Hartwick College
in New York, for her expert review of the manuscript.

Copyright © 2011 Marshall Cavendish Corporation

Published by Marshall Cavendish Benchmark
An imprint of Marshall Cavendish Corporation

Other Marshall Cavendish Offices:
Marshall Cavendish International (Asia) Private Limited, 1 New Industrial Road, Singapore 536196 • Marshall
Cavendish International (Thailand) Co Ltd. 253 Asoke, 12th Flr, Sukhumvit 21 Road, Klongtoey Nua, Wattana,
Bangkok 10110, Thailand • Marshall Cavendish (Malaysia) Sdn Bhd, Times Subang, Lot 46, Subang Hi-Tech
Industrial Park, Batu Tiga, 40000 Shah Alam, Selangor Darul Ehsan, Malaysia

Marshall Cavendish is a trademark of Times Publishing Limited
All websites were available and accurate when this book was sent to press.

Library of Congress Cataloguing-in-Publication Data
Naden, Corinne J.
The taming of the shrew / by Corinne J. Naden.
p. cm. — (Shakespeare explained)
Includes bibliographical references and index.
Summary: "A literary analysis of the play 'The Taming of the Shrew.' Includes information on the history and
culture of Elizabethan England"--Provided by publisher.
ISBN 978-1-60870-019-6
1. Shakespeare, William, 1564-1616. Taming of the shrew—Juvenile literature. I. Title.
PR2832.N33 2011
822.3'3—dc22
2009041728

Photo research by: Linda Sykes
The photographs in this book are used by permission and through the courtesy of: Nigel Norrington/
ArenaPAL/Topfoto/The Image Works: front cover; Jordan Chesbrough/istockphoto: 1; Mikhali/Shutterstock:
2-3; Neven Mendrila/Shutterstock: 3, 39 (right), 47 (right), 95 (right); Raciro/istockphoto: 4, 40, 48, 96, back
cover; Art Parts RF: 6, 8, 13, 26, 27, 34; ©Nik Wheeler/Corbis: 11; Portraitgalerie, Schloss Ambras, Innsbruck,
Austria/Erich Lessing/Art Resource, NY: 20; Travelshots.com/Alamy: 22; ©Hideo Kurihara/Alamy: 24; Corbis/
Sygma: 29; Andrew Fox/Corbis: 32; Allposters.com: 39; Copyright Utah Shakespearean Festival. Photo by Karl
Hugh: 43, 62, 100, 104; Royal File International/F.A.I. Productions/The Everett Collection: 47; Nigel Norrington/
ArenaPAL/Topfoto/The Image Works: 52; The Everett Collection: 55, 95; Pictorial Press Ltd./Alamy: 67;
Newscom: 77; Elliott Franks/ArenaPAL/Topfoto/The Image Works: 86; United Archives GmbH/Alamy: 90.

Editor: Megan Comerford
Publisher: Michelle Bisson
Art Director: Anahid Hamparian
Series Design: Kay Petronio

Printed in Malaysia (T)
135642

Contents

Shakespeare and His World

WILLIAM SHAKESPEARE, OFTEN NICKNAMED "THE BARD," IS, BEYOND ANY COMPARISON, THE MOST TOWERING NAME IN ENGLISH LITERATURE. MANY CONSIDER HIS PLAYS THE GREATEST EVER WRITTEN. HE STANDS OUT EVEN AMONG GENIUSES.

Yet the Bard is also closer to our hearts than lesser writers, and his tremendous reputation should neither intimidate us nor prevent us from enjoying the simple delights he offers in such abundance. It is as if he had written for each of us personally. As he himself put it, "One touch of nature makes the whole world kin."

Such tragedies as *Hamlet*, *Romeo and Juliet*, and *Macbeth* are world famous, still performed onstage and in films. These and other plays have also been adapted for radio, television, opera, ballet, pantomime, novels, comic books, and other media. Two of the best ways to become familiar with them are to watch some of the many fine movies that have been made of them and to listen to recordings of them by some of the world's great actors.

Even Shakespeare's individual characters have lives of their own, like real historical figures. Hamlet is still regarded as the most challenging role ever written for an actor. Roughly as many whole books have been written about Hamlet, an imaginary character, as about actual historical figures such as Abraham Lincoln and Napoleon Bonaparte.

Shakespeare created an amazing variety of vivid characters. One of Shakespeare's most peculiar traits was that he loved his characters so much—even some of his villains and secondary or comic characters—that at times he let them run away with the play, stealing attention from his heroes and heroines.

So in *A Midsummer Night's Dream* audiences remember the absurd and lovable fool Bottom the Weaver better than the lovers who are the main characters. Romeo's friend Mercutio is more fiery and witty than Romeo himself; legend claims that Shakespeare said he had to kill Mercutio or Mercutio would have killed the play.

Shakespeare also wrote dozens of comedies and historical plays, as well as nondramatic poems. Although his tragedies are now regarded as his greatest works, he freely mixed them with comedy and history. And his sonnets are among the supreme love poems in the English language.

It is Shakespeare's mastery of the English language that keeps his words familiar to us today. Every literate person knows dramatic lines such as "Wherefore art thou Romeo?"; "My kingdom for a horse!"; "To be or not to be: that is the question"; "Friends, Romans, countrymen, lend me your ears"; and "What fools these mortals be!" Shakespeare's sonnets are noted for their sweetness: "Shall I compare thee to a summer's day?"

I WOULD NOT WED HER FOR A MINE OF GOLD

SHAKESPEARE'S LANGUAGE

WITHOUT A DOUBT, SHAKESPEARE WAS THE GREATEST MASTER OF THE ENGLISH LANGUAGE WHO EVER LIVED. BUT JUST WHAT DOES THAT MEAN?

Shakespeare's vocabulary was huge, full of references to the Bible as well as Greek and Roman mythology. Yet his most brilliant phrases often combine very simple and familiar words:

"WHAT'S IN A NAME? THAT WHICH WE CALL A ROSE BY ANY OTHER NAME WOULD SMELL AS SWEET."

He has delighted countless millions of readers. And we know him only through his language. He has shaped modern English far more than any other writer.

Or, to put it in more personal terms, you probably quote his words several times every day without realizing it, even if you have never suspected that Shakespeare could be a source of pleasure to you.

So why do so many English-speaking readers find his language so difficult? It is our language, too, but it has changed so much that it is no longer quite the same language—nor a completely different one, either.

Shakespeare's English and ours overlap without being identical. He would have some difficulty understanding us, too! Many of our everyday words and phrases would baffle him.

Shakespeare, for example, would not know what we meant by a *car,* a *radio,* a *movie,* a *television,* a *computer,* or a *sitcom,* since these things did not even exist in his time. Our old-fashioned term *railroad train* would be unimaginable to him, far in the distant future. We would have to explain to him (if we could) what *nuclear weapons, electricity,* and *democracy* are. He would also be a little puzzled by common expressions such as *high-tech, feel the heat, approval ratings, war criminal, judgmental,* and *whoopee cushion.*

So how can we call him "the greatest master of the English language"? It might seem as if he barely spoke English at all! (He would, however, recognize much of our dirty slang, even if he pronounced it slightly differently. His plays also contain many racial insults to Jews, Africans, Italians, Irish, and others. Today he would be called "insensitive.")

Many of the words of Shakespeare's time have become archaic. Words like *thou, thee, thy, thyself,* and *thine,* which were among the most common words in the language in Shakespeare's day, have all but disappeared today. We simply say *you* for both singular and plural, formal and familiar. Most other modern languages have kept their *thou.*

Sometimes the same words now have different meanings. We are apt to be misled by such simple, familiar words as *kind, wonderful, waste, just,* and *dear,* which he often uses in ways that differ from our usage.

Shakespeare also doesn't always use the words we expect to hear, the words that we ourselves would naturally use. When we might automatically say, "I beg your pardon" or just "Sorry," he might say, "I cry you mercy."

Often a glossary and footnotes will solve all three of these problems for us. But it is most important to bear in mind that Shakespeare was often hard for his first audiences to understand. Even in his own time his rich language was challenging. And this was deliberate. Shakespeare was inventing his own kind of English. It remains unique today.

A child doesn't learn to talk by using a dictionary. Children learn first by sheer immersion. We teach babies by pointing at things and saying their names. Yet the toddler always learns faster than we can teach! Even as babies we are geniuses. Dictionaries can help us later, when we already speak and read the language well (and learn more slowly).

So the best way to learn Shakespeare is not to depend on the footnotes and glossary too much, but instead to be like a baby: just get into the flow of the language. Go to performances of the plays or watch movies of them.

THE LANGUAGE HAS A MAGICAL WAY OF TEACHING ITSELF, IF WE LET IT. THERE IS NO REASON TO FEEL STUPID OR FRUSTRATED WHEN IT DOESN'T COME EASILY.

Hundreds of phrases have entered the English language from *Hamlet* alone, including "to hold, as 'twere, the mirror up to nature"; "murder most foul"; "the thousand natural shocks that flesh is heir to"; "flaming youth"; "a countenance more in sorrow than in anger"; "the play's the thing"; "neither a borrower nor a lender be"; "in my mind's eye"; "something is rotten in the state of Denmark"; "alas, poor Yorick"; and "the lady doth protest too much, methinks."

From other plays we get the phrases "star-crossed lovers"; "what's in a name?"; "we have scotched the snake, not killed it"; "one fell swoop"; "it was Greek to me"; "I come to bury Caesar, not to praise him"; and "the most unkindest cut of all"—all these are among our household words. In fact, Shakespeare even gave us the expression "household words." No wonder his contemporaries marveled at his "fine filed phrase" and swooned at the "mellifluous and honey-tongued Shakespeare."

Shakespeare's words seem to combine music, magic, wisdom, and humor:

"THE COURSE OF TRUE LOVE NEVER DID RUN SMOOTH."

"HE JESTS AT SCARS THAT NEVER FELT A WOUND."

"THE FAULT, DEAR BRUTUS, IS NOT IN OUR STARS, BUT IN OURSELVES, THAT WE ARE UNDERLINGS."

"COWARDS DIE MANY TIMES BEFORE THEIR DEATHS; THE VALIANT NEVER TASTE OF DEATH BUT ONCE."

"NOT THAT I LOVED CAESAR LESS, BUT THAT I LOVED ROME MORE."

"THERE ARE MORE THINGS IN HEAVEN AND EARTH, HORATIO, THAN ARE DREAMT OF IN YOUR PHILOSOPHY."

"BREVITY IS THE SOUL OF WIT."

"THERE'S A DIVINITY THAT SHAPES OUR ENDS, ROUGH-HEW THEM HOW WE WILL."

Four centuries after Shakespeare lived, to speak English is to quote him. His huge vocabulary and linguistic fertility are still astonishing. He has had a powerful effect on all of us, whether we realize it or not. We may wonder how it is even possible for a single human being to say so many memorable things.

Only the King James translation of the Bible, perhaps, has had a more profound and pervasive influence on the English language than Shakespeare. And, of course, the Bible was written by many authors over many centuries, and the King James translation, published in 1611, was the combined effort of many scholars.

EARLY LIFE

So who, exactly, was Shakespeare? Mystery surrounds his life, largely because few records were kept during his time. Some people have even doubted his identity, arguing that the real author of Shakespeare's plays must have been a man of superior formal education and wide experience. In a sense such doubts are a natural and understandable reaction to his rare, almost miraculous powers of expression, but some people feel that the doubts themselves show a lack of respect for the supremely human poet.

Most scholars agree that Shakespeare was born in the town of Stratford-upon-Avon in the county of Warwickshire, England, in April 1564. He was baptized, according to local church records, Gulielmus (William) Shakspere (the name was spelled in several different ways) on April 26 of that year. He was one of several children, most of whom died young.

His father, John Shakespeare (or Shakspere), was a glove maker and, at times, a town official. He was often in debt or being fined for unknown delinquencies, perhaps failure to attend church regularly. It is suspected that John was a recusant (secret and illegal) Catholic, but there is no proof. Many

scholars have found Catholic tendencies in Shakespeare's plays, but whether Shakespeare was Catholic or not we can only guess.

At the time of Shakespeare's birth, England was torn by religious controversy and persecution. The country had left the Roman Catholic Church during the reign of King Henry VIII, who had died in 1547. Two of Henry's children, Edward and Mary, ruled after his death. When his daughter Elizabeth I became queen in 1558, she upheld his claim that the monarch of England was also head of the English Church.

Did William attend the local grammar school? He was probably entitled to, given his father's prominence in Stratford, but again, we face a frustrating absence of proof, and many people of the time learned to read very well without schooling. If he went to the town school, he would also have learned the rudiments of Latin.

We know very little about the first half of William's life. In 1582, when he was eighteen, he married Anne Hathaway, eight years his senior. Their first daughter, Susanna, was born six months later. The following year they had twins, Hamnet and Judith.

At this point William disappears from the records again. By the early 1590s we find "William Shakespeare" in London, a member of the city's leading acting company, called the Lord Chamberlain's Men. Many of Shakespeare's greatest roles, we are told, were first performed by the company's star, Richard Burbage.

Curiously, the first work published under (and identified with) Shakespeare's name was not a play but a long erotic poem, *Venus and Adonis*, in 1593. It was dedicated to the young Earl of Southampton, Henry Wriothesley.

Venus and Adonis was a spectacular success, and Shakespeare was immediately hailed as a major poet. In 1594 he dedicated a longer, more serious poem to Southampton, *The Rape of Lucrece*. It was another hit, and for many years, these two poems were considered Shakespeare's greatest works, despite the popularity of his plays.

"WHAT, IS THE MAN A LUNATIC?"

TODAY MOVIES, NOT LIVE PLAYS, ARE THE MORE POPULAR ART FORM. FORTUNATELY MOST OF SHAKESPEARE'S PLAYS HAVE BEEN FILMED, AND THE BEST OF THESE MOVIES OFFER AN EXCELLENT WAY TO MAKE THE BARD'S ACQUAINTANCE. RECENTLY, KENNETH BRANAGH HAS BECOME A RESPECTED CONVERTER OF SHAKESPEARE'S PLAYS INTO FILM.

As You Like It

One of the earliest screen versions of *As You Like It* is the 1936 film starring Laurence Olivier as Orlando and Elisabeth Bergner as Rosalind. The *New York Times*, in a movie review, praised both the directorial interpretation and the actors' portrayals. British actress Helen Mirren starred in a 1978 BBC production that was filmed entirely outdoors. The most recent film version, directed by renowned Shakespearean actor Kenneth Branagh, aired in 2006 on HBO. Set in nineteenth-century Japan, it is visually stunning and a decent interpretation of the play. It also boasts an impressive supporting cast, including Kevin Kline as Jaques, Alfred Molina as Touchstone, and Romola Garai as Celia.

Hamlet

Hamlet, Shakespeare's most famous play, has been well filmed several times. In 1948 Laurence Olivier won three Academy

Awards—for best picture, best actor, and best director—for his version of the play. The film allowed him to show some of the magnetism that made him famous on the stage. Nobody spoke Shakespeare's lines more thrillingly.

The young Derek Jacobi played Hamlet in a 1980 BBC production of the play, with Patrick Stewart (now best known for *Star Trek: The Next Generation*) as the guilty king. Jacobi, like Olivier, has a gift for speaking the lines freshly; he never seems to be merely reciting the famous and familiar words. But whereas Olivier has animal passion, Jacobi is more intellectual. It is fascinating to compare the ways these two outstanding actors play Shakespeare's most complex character.

Franco Zeffirelli's 1990 *Hamlet*, starring Mel Gibson, is fascinating in a different way. Gibson, of course, is best known as an action hero, and he is not well suited to this supremely witty and introspective role, but Zeffirelli cuts the text drastically, and the result turns *Hamlet* into something that few people would have expected: a short, swiftly moving action movie. Several of the other characters are brilliantly played.

Henry IV, Part One

The 1979 BBC Shakespeare series production does a commendable job in this straightforward approach to the play. Battle scenes are effective despite obvious restrictions in an indoor studio setting. Anthony Quayle gives jovial Falstaff a darker edge, and Tim Pigott-Smith's Hotspur is buoyed by some humor. Jon Finch plays King Henry IV with noble authority, and David Gwillim gives Hal a surprisingly successful transformation from boy prince to heir apparent.

Julius Caesar

No really good movie of *Julius Caesar* exists, but the 1953 film, with Marlon Brando as Mark Antony, will do. James Mason is a thoughtful Brutus, and John Gielgud, then ranked with Laurence Olivier among the greatest Shakespearean actors, plays the villainous Cassius. The film is rather dull, and Brando is out of place in a Roman toga, but it is still worth viewing.

King Lear

In the past century, *King Lear* has been adapted for film approximately fifteen times. Peter Brook directed a bleak 1971 version starring British actor Paul Scofield as Lear. One of the best film versions of *King Lear*, not surprisingly, features Laurence Olivier in the title role. The 1983 British TV version, directed by Michael Elliott, provides a straightforward interpretation of the play, though the visual quality may seem dated to the twenty-first–century viewer. Olivier won an Emmy for Outstanding Lead Actor for his role.

Macbeth

Roman Polanski is best known as a director of thrillers and horror films, so it may seem natural that he should have done his 1971 *The Tragedy of Macbeth* as an often-gruesome slasher flick. But this is also one of the most vigorous of all Shakespeare films. Macbeth and his wife are played by Jon Finch and Francesca Annis, neither known for playing Shakespeare, but they are young and attractive in roles that are usually given to older actors, which gives the story a fresh flavor.

The Merchant of Venice

Once again the matchless Sir Laurence Olivier delivers a great performance as Shylock with his wife Joan Plowright as Portia in the 1974 TV film, adapted from the 1970 National Theater (of Britain) production. A 1980 BBC offering features Warren Mitchell as Shylock and Gemma Jones as Portia, with John Rhys-Davies as Salerio. The most recent production, starring Al Pacino as Shylock, Jeremy Irons as Antonio, and Joseph Fiennes as Bassanio, was filmed in Venice and released in 2004.

A Midsummer Night's Dream

Because of the prestige of his tragedies, we tend to forget how many comedies Shakespeare wrote—nearly twice the number of tragedies. Of these perhaps the most popular has always been the enchanting, atmospheric, and very silly masterpiece *A Midsummer Night's Dream*.

Several films have been made of *A Midsummer Night's Dream*. Among the more notable have been Max Reinhardt's 1935 black-and-white version, with Mickey Rooney (then a child star) as Puck.

Of the several film versions, the one starring Kevin Kline as Bottom and Stanley Tucci as Puck, made in 1999 with nineteenth-century costumes and directed by Michael Hoffman, ranks among the finest, and is surely one of the most sumptuous to watch.

Othello

Orson Welles did a budget European version in 1952, now available as a restored DVD. Laurence Olivier's 1965 film performance is predictably remarkable, though it has been said that he would only approach the part by honoring, even emulating, Paul Robeson's definitive interpretation that ran on Broadway in 1943. (Robeson was the first black actor to play Othello, the Moor of Venice, and he did so to critical acclaim, though sadly his performance was never filmed.) Maggie Smith plays a formidable Desdemona opposite Olivier, and her youth and energy will surprise younger audiences who know her only from the *Harry Potter* films. Laurence Fishburne brilliantly portrayed Othello in the 1995 film, costarring with Kenneth Branagh as a surprisingly human Iago, though Irène Jacob's Desdemona was disappointingly weak.

Richard III

Many well-known actors have portrayed the villainous Richard III on film. Of course, Laurence Olivier stepped in to play the role of Richard in a 1955 version he also directed. Director Richard Loncraine chose to set his 1995 film version in Nazi Germany. The movie, which starred Ian McKellen as Richard, was nominated for two Oscars; McKellen was nominated for a Golden Globe for his performance. The World War II interpretation also featured Robert Downey Jr. as Rivers, Kristin Scott Thomas as Lady Anne, and Maggie Smith (from the *Harry Potter* movies) as the Duchess of York. A 2008 version, directed by and starring Scott Anderson, is set in modern-day Los Angeles. Prolific actor David Carradine portrays Buckingham.

Romeo and Juliet

This, the world's most famous love story, has been filmed many times, twice very successfully over the last generation. Franco Zeffirelli directed a hit version in 1968 with Leonard Whiting and the rapturously pretty Olivia Hussey, set in Renaissance Italy. Baz

Luhrmann made a much more contemporary version, with a loud rock score, starring Leonardo DiCaprio and Claire Danes, in 1996.

It seems safe to say that Shakespeare would have preferred Zeffirelli's movie, with its superior acting and rich, romantic, sun-drenched Italian scenery.

The Taming of the Shrew

Franco Zeffirelli's 1967 film version of *The Taming of the Shrew* starred Elizabeth Taylor as Kate and Richard Burton as Petruchio. Shakespeare's original lines were significantly cut and altered to accommodate both the film media and Taylor's inexperience as a Shakespearean actress.

Gil Junger's 1999 movie *10 Things I Hate About You* is loosely based on Shakespeare's play. Julia Stiles and Heath Ledger star in this interpretation set in a modern-day high school. In 2005 BBC aired a version of Shakespeare's play set in twenty-first-century England. Kate is a successful, driven politician who succumbs to cash-strapped Petruchio, played by Rufus Sewell.

The Tempest

A 1960 Hallmark Hall of Fame production featured Maurice Evans as Prospero, Lee Remick as Miranda, Roddy McDowall as Ariel, and Richard Burton as Caliban. The special effects are primitive and the costumes are ludicrous, but it moves along at a fast pace. Another TV version aired in 1998 and was nominated for a Golden Globe. Peter Fonda played Gideon Prosper, and Katherine Heigl played his daughter Miranda Prosper. Sci-fi fans may already know that the classic 1956 film *Forbidden Planet* is modeled on themes and characters from the play.

Twelfth Night

Trevor Nunn adapted the play for the 1996 film he also directed in a rapturous Edwardian setting, with big names like Helena Bonham Carter, Richard E. Grant, Imogen Stubbs, and Ben Kingsley as Feste. A 2003 film set in modern Britain provides an interesting multicultural experience; it features an Anglo-Indian cast with Parminder Nagra (*Bend It Like Beckham*) playing Viola. For the truly intrepid, a twelve-minute silent film made in 1910 does a fine job of capturing the play through visual gags and over-the-top gesturing.

THESE FILMS HAVE BEEN SELECTED FOR SEVERAL QUALITIES: APPEAL AND ACCESSIBILITY TO MODERN AUDIENCES, EXCELLENCE IN ACTING, PACING, VISUAL BEAUTY, AND, OF COURSE, FIDELITY TO SHAKESPEARE. THEY ARE THE MOTION PICTURES WE JUDGE MOST LIKELY TO HELP STUDENTS UNDERSTAND THE SOURCE OF THE BARD'S LASTING POWER.

SHAKESPEARE'S THEATER

Today we sometimes speak of "live entertainment." In Shakespeare's day, of course, all entertainment was live, because recordings, films, television, and radio did not yet exist. Even printed books were a novelty.

In fact, most communication in those days was difficult. Transportation was not only difficult but slow, chiefly by horse and boat. Most people were illiterate peasants who lived on farms that they seldom left; cities grew up along waterways and were subject to frequent plagues that could wipe out much of the population within weeks.

Money—in coin form, not paper—was scarce and hardly existed outside the cities. By today's standards, even the rich were poor. Life was precarious. Most children died young, and famine or disease might kill anyone at any time. Everyone was familiar with death. Starvation was not rare or remote, as it is to most of us today. Medical care was poor and might kill as many people as it healed.

This was the grim background of Shakespeare's theater during the reign of Queen Elizabeth I, who ruled from 1558 until her death in 1603. During that period England was also torn by religious conflict, often violent, among Roman Catholics who were

ELIZABETH I, A GREAT PATRON OF POETRY AND THE THEATER, WROTE SONNETS AND TRANSLATED CLASSIC WORKS.

loyal to the pope, adherents of the Church of England who were loyal to the queen, and the Puritans who would take over the country in the revolution of 1642.

Under these conditions, most forms of entertainment were luxuries that were out of most people's reach. The only way to hear music was to be in the actual physical presence of singers or musicians with their instruments, which were primitive by our standards.

One brutal form of entertainment, popular in London, was bearbaiting. A bear was blinded and chained to a stake, where fierce dogs called mastiffs were turned loose to tear him apart. The theaters had to compete with the bear gardens, as they were called, for spectators.

The Puritans, or radical Protestants, objected to bearbaiting and tried to ban it. Despite their modern reputation, the Puritans were anything but conservative. Conservative people, attached to old customs, hated the Puritans. They seemed to upset everything. (Many of America's first settlers, such as the Pilgrims who came over on the *Mayflower*, were dissidents who were fleeing the Church of England.)

Plays were extremely popular, but they were primitive, too. They had to be performed outdoors in the afternoon because of the lack of indoor lighting. Often the "theater" was only an enclosed courtyard. Probably the versions of Shakespeare's plays that we know today were not used in full, but shortened to about two hours for actual performance.

But eventually more regular theaters were built, featuring a raised stage extending into the audience. Poorer spectators (illiterate "groundlings") stood on the ground around it, at times exposed to rain and snow. Wealthier people sat in raised tiers above. Aside from some costumes, there were few props or special effects and almost no scenery. Much had to be imagined: Whole battles might be represented by a few actors with swords. Thunder might be simulated by rattling a sheet of tin offstage.

The plays were far from realistic and, under the conditions of the time, could hardly try to be. Above the rear of the main stage was a small balcony. (It was this balcony from which Juliet spoke to Romeo.) Ghosts and witches might appear by entering through a trapdoor in the stage floor.

Unlike the modern theater, Shakespeare's Globe Theater—he describes it as "this wooden O"—had no curtain separating the stage from the audience. This allowed intimacy between the players and the spectators.

THE RECONSTRUCTED GLOBE THEATER WAS COMPLETED IN 1997 AND IS LOCATED IN LONDON, JUST 200 YARDS (183 METERS) FROM THE SITE OF THE ORIGINAL.

IT IS THE RIVAL OF MY LOVE.

The spectators probably reacted rowdily to the play, not listening in reverent silence. After all, they had come to have fun! And few of them were scholars. Again, a play had to amuse people who could not read.

The lines of plays were written and spoken in prose or, more often, in a form of verse called iambic pentameter (ten syllables with five stresses per line). There was no attempt at modern realism. Only males were allowed on the stage, so some of the greatest women's roles ever written had to be played by boys or men. (The same is true, by the way, of the ancient Greek theater.)

Actors had to be versatile, skilled not only in acting, but also in fencing, singing, dancing, and acrobatics. Within its limitations, the theater offered a considerable variety of spectacles.

Plays were big business, not yet regarded as high art, sponsored by important and powerful people (the queen loved them as much as the groundlings did). The London acting companies also toured and performed in the provinces. When plagues struck London, the government might order the theaters to be closed to prevent the spread of disease among crowds. (They remained empty for nearly two years from 1593 to 1594.)

As the theater became more popular, the Puritans grew as hostile to it as they were to bearbaiting. Plays, like books, were censored by the government, and the Puritans fought to increase restrictions, eventually banning any mention of God and other sacred topics on the stage.

In 1642 the Puritans shut down all the theaters in London, and in 1644 they had the Globe demolished. The theaters remained closed until Charles's son, King Charles II, was restored to the throne in 1660 and the hated Puritans were finally vanquished.

But, by then, the tradition of Shakespeare's theater had been fatally interrupted. His plays remained popular, but they were often rewritten by inferior dramatists, and it was many years before they were performed (again) as he had originally written them.

THE ROYAL SHAKESPEARE THEATER, IN STRATFORD-UPON-AVON, WAS CLOSED IN 2007 TO BUILD A 1,000-SEAT AUDITORIUM.

Today, of course, the plays are performed both in theaters and in films, sometimes in costumes of the period (ancient Rome for *Julius Caesar*, medieval England for *Henry V*), sometimes in modern dress (*Richard III* has recently been reset in England in the 1930s).

PLAYS

In the England of Queen Elizabeth I, plays were enjoyed by all classes of people, but they were not yet respected as a serious form of art.

Shakespeare's plays began to appear in print in individual, or quarto, editions in 1594, but none of these bore his name until 1598. Although his tragedies are now ranked as his supreme achievements, his name was first associated with comedies and with plays about English history.

The dates of Shakespeare's plays are notoriously hard to determine. Few performances of them were documented; some were not printed until decades after they first appeared on the stage. Mainstream scholars generally place most of the comedies and histories in the 1590s, admitting that this time frame is no more than a widely accepted estimate.

The three parts of *King Henry VI*, culminating in a fourth part, *Richard III*, deal with the long and complex dynastic struggle or civil wars known as the Wars of the Roses (1455–1487), one of England's most turbulent periods. Today it is not easy to follow the plots of these plays.

It may seem strange to us that a young playwright should have written such demanding works early in his career, but they were evidently very popular with the Elizabethan public. Of the four, only *Richard III*, with its wonderfully villainous starring role, is still often performed.

Even today, one of Shakespeare's early comedies, *The Taming of the Shrew*, remains a crowd-pleaser. (It has enjoyed success in a 1999 film adaptation, *10 Things I Hate About You,* with Heath Ledger and Julia Stiles.) The story is simple: The enterprising Petruchio resolves to marry a rich

THE "REAL" SHAKESPEARE

AROUND 1850 DOUBTS STARTED TO SURFACE ABOUT WHO HAD ACTUALLY WRITTEN SHAKESPEARE'S PLAYS, CHIEFLY BECAUSE MANY OTHER AUTHORS, SUCH AS MARK TWAIN, THOUGHT THE PLAYS' AUTHOR WAS TOO WELL EDUCATED AND KNOWLEDGEABLE TO HAVE BEEN THE MODESTLY SCHOOLED MAN FROM STRATFORD.

Who, then, was the real author? Many answers have been given, but the three leading candidates are Francis Bacon, Christopher Marlowe, and Edward de Vere, Earl of Oxford.

Francis Bacon (1561-1626)

Bacon was a distinguished lawyer, scientist, philosopher, and essayist. Many considered him one of the great geniuses of his time, capable of any literary achievement, though he wrote little poetry and, as far as we know, no dramas. When people began to suspect that "Shakespeare" was only a pen name, he seemed like a natural candidate. But his writing style was vastly different from the style of the plays.

Christopher Marlowe (1564–1593)

Marlowe wrote several excellent tragedies in a style much like that of the Shakespearean tragedies, though without the comic blend. But he was reportedly killed in a mysterious incident in 1593, before most of the Bard's plays existed. Could his death have been faked? Is it possible that he lived on for decades in hiding, writing under a pen name? This is what his advocates contend.

Edward de Vere, Earl of Oxford (1550–1604)

Oxford is now the most popular and plausible alternative to the lad from Stratford. He had a high reputation as a poet and playwright in his day, but his life was full of scandal. That controversial life seems to match what the poet says about himself in the sonnets, as well as many events in the plays (especially *Hamlet*). However, he died in 1604, and most scholars believe this rules him out as the author of plays that were published after that date.

THE GREAT MAJORITY OF EXPERTS REJECT THESE AND ALL OTHER ALTERNATIVE CANDIDATES, STICKING WITH THE TRADITIONAL VIEW, AFFIRMED IN THE 1623 FIRST FOLIO OF THE PLAYS, THAT THE AUTHOR WAS THE MAN FROM STRATFORD. THAT REMAINS THE SAFEST POSITION TO TAKE, UNLESS STARTLING NEW EVIDENCE TURNS UP, WHICH, AT THIS LATE DATE, SEEMS HIGHLY UNLIKELY.

young woman, Katherina Minola, for her wealth, despite her reputation for having a bad temper. Nothing she does can discourage this dauntless suitor, and the play ends with Kate becoming a submissive wife. It is all the funnier for being unbelievable.

With *Romeo and Juliet* the Bard created his first enduring triumph. This tragedy of "star-crossed lovers" from feuding families is known around the world. Even people with only the vaguest knowledge of Shakespeare are often aware of this universally beloved story. It has inspired countless similar stories and adaptations, such as the hit musical *West Side Story*.

By the mid-1590s Shakespeare was successful and prosperous, a partner in the Lord Chamberlain's Men. He was rich enough to buy New Place, one of the largest houses in his hometown of Stratford.

Yet, at the peak of his good fortune came the worst sorrow of his life: Hamnet, his only son, died in August 1596 at the age of eleven, leaving nobody to carry on his family name, which was to die out with his two daughters.

Our only evidence of his son's death is a single line in the parish burial register. As far as we know, this crushing loss left no mark on Shakespeare's work. As far as his creative life shows, it was as if nothing had happened. His silence about his grief may be the greatest puzzle of his mysterious life, although, as we shall see, others remain.

During this period, according to traditional dating (even if it must be somewhat hypothetical), came the torrent of Shakespeare's mightiest works. Among these was another quartet of English history plays, this one centering on the legendary King Henry IV, including *Richard II* and the two parts of *Henry IV*.

Then came a series of wonderful romantic comedies: *Much Ado About Nothing*, *As You Like It*, and *Twelfth Night*.

In 1598 the clergyman Francis Meres, as part of a larger work, hailed

Shakespeare as the English Ovid, supreme in love poetry as well as drama. "The Muses would speak with Shakespeare's fine filed phrase," Meres wrote, "if they would speak English." He added praise of Shakespeare's "sugared sonnets among his private friends." It is tantalizing; Meres seems to know something of the poet's personal life, but he gives us no hard information. No wonder biographers are frustrated.

Next the Bard returned gloriously to tragedy with *Julius Caesar*. In the play Caesar has returned to Rome in great popularity after his military triumphs. Brutus and several other leading senators, suspecting that Caesar means to make himself king, plot to assassinate him. Midway through the play, after the assassination, comes one of Shakespeare's most famous scenes. Brutus speaks at Caesar's funeral. But then Caesar's friend Mark Antony delivers a powerful attack on the conspirators, inciting the mob to fury. Brutus and the others, forced to flee Rome, die in the ensuing civil war. In the end the spirit of Caesar wins after all. If Shakespeare had written nothing after *Julius Caesar*, he would still have been remembered as one of the greatest playwrights of all time. But his supreme works were still to come.

Only Shakespeare could have surpassed *Julius Caesar*, and he did so with *Hamlet* (usually dated about 1600). King Hamlet of Denmark has died, apparently bitten by a poisonous snake. Claudius, his brother, has married the dead king's widow, Gertrude, and become the new king, to the disgust and horror of Prince Hamlet. The ghost of old Hamlet appears to young Hamlet, reveals that he was actually poisoned by Claudius, and demands revenge. Hamlet accepts this as his duty, but cannot bring himself to kill his hated uncle. What follows is Shakespeare's most brilliant and controversial plot.

The story of *Hamlet* is set against the religious controversies of the Bard's time. Is the ghost in hell or purgatory? Is Hamlet Catholic or Protestant? Can revenge ever be justified? We are never really given the answers to such questions. But the play reverberates with them.

THE KING'S MEN

In 1603 Queen Elizabeth I died, and King James VI of Scotland became King James I of England. He also became the patron of Shakespeare's acting company, so the Lord Chamberlain's Men became the King's Men. From this point on, we know less of Shakespeare's life in London than in Stratford, where he kept acquiring property.

In the later years of the sixteenth century Shakespeare had been a rather elusive figure in London, delinquent in paying taxes. From 1602 to 1604 he lived, according to his own later testimony, with a French immigrant family named Mountjoy. After 1604 there is no record of any London residence for Shakespeare, nor do we have any reliable recollection of him or his whereabouts by others. As always, the documents leave much to be desired.

Nearly as great as *Hamlet* is *Othello*, and many regard *King Lear*, the heartbreaking tragedy about an old king and his three daughters, as Shakespeare's supreme tragedy. Shakespeare's shortest tragedy, *Macbeth*, tells the story of a Scottish lord and his wife who plot to murder the king of Scotland to gain the throne for themselves. *Antony and Cleopatra*, a sequel to *Julius Caesar*, depicts the aging Mark Antony in love with the enchanting queen of Egypt. *Coriolanus*, another Roman tragedy, is the poet's least popular masterpiece.

SONNETS AND THE END

The year 1609 saw the publication of Shakespeare's Sonnets. Of these 154 puzzling love poems, the first 126 are addressed to a handsome young man, unnamed, but widely believed to be the Earl of Southampton; the rest concern a dark woman, also unidentified. These mysteries are still debated by scholars.

Near the end of his career Shakespeare turned to comedy again, but it was a comedy of a new and more serious kind. Magic plays a large role in these late plays. For example, in *The Tempest*, the exiled duke of Milan, Prospero, uses magic to defeat his enemies and bring about a final reconciliation.

According to the most commonly accepted view, Shakespeare, not yet fifty, retired to Stratford around 1610. He died prosperous in 1616 and left a will that divided his goods, with a famous provision leaving his wife "my second-best bed." He was buried in the chancel of the parish church, under a tombstone bearing a crude rhyme:

GOOD FRIEND, FOR JESUS SAKE FORBEARE,
TO DIG THE DUST ENCLOSED HERE.
BLEST BE THE MAN THAT SPARES THESE STONES,
AND CURSED BE HE THAT MOVES MY BONES.

This epitaph is another hotly debated mystery: did the great poet actually compose these lines himself?

SHAKESPEARE'S GRAVE IN HOLY TRINITY CHURCH, STRATFORD-UPON-AVON. HIS WIFE, ANNE HATHAWAY, IS BURIED BESIDE HIM.

THE FOLIO

In 1623 Shakespeare's colleagues of the King's Men produced a large volume of the plays (excluding the sonnets and other poems) titled *Mr. William Shakespeares Comedies, Histories, & Tragedies* with a woodcut portrait of the Bard. As a literary monument it is priceless, containing our only texts of half the plays; as a source of biographical information it is severely disappointing, giving not even the dates of Shakespeare's birth and death.

Ben Jonson, then England's poet laureate, supplied a long prefatory poem saluting Shakespeare as the equal of the great classical Greek tragedians Aeschylus, Sophocles, and Euripides, adding that "He was not of an age, but for all time."

Some would later denigrate Shakespeare. His reputation took more than a century to conquer Europe, where many regarded him as semi-barbarous. His works were not translated before 1740. Jonson himself, despite his personal affection, would deprecate "idolatry" of the Bard. For a time Jonson himself was considered more "correct" than Shakespeare, and possibly the superior artist.

But Jonson's generous verdict is now the whole world's. Shakespeare was not merely of his own age, "but for all time."

I KNOW SHE IS AN IRKSOME, BRAWLING SCOLD.

A GLOSSARY OF LITERARY TERMS

allegory—a story in which characters and events stand for general moral truths. Shakespeare never uses this form simply, but his plays are full of allegorical elements.

alliteration—repetition of one or more initial sounds, especially consonants, as in the saying "through thick and thin," or in Julius Caesar's statement, "veni, vidi, vici."

allusion—a reference, especially when the subject referred to is not actually named, but is unmistakably hinted at.

aside—a short speech in which a character speaks to the audience, unheard by other characters on the stage.

comedy—a story written to amuse, using devices such as witty dialogue (high comedy) or silly physical movement (low comedy). Most of Shakespeare's comedies were romantic comedies, incorporating lovers who endure separations, misunderstandings, and other obstacles but who are finally united in a happy resolution.

deus ex machina—an unexpected, artificial resolution to a play's convoluted plot. Literally, "god out of a machine."

dialogue—speech that takes place among two or more characters.

diction—choice of words for a given tone. A speech's diction may be dignified (as when a king formally addresses his court), comic (as when the ignorant grave diggers debate whether Ophelia deserves a religious funeral), vulgar, romantic, or whatever the dramatic occasion requires. Shakespeare was a master of diction.

Elizabethan—having to do with the reign of Queen Elizabeth I, from 1558 until her death in 1603. This is considered the most famous period in the history of England, chiefly because of Shakespeare and other noted authors (among them Sir Philip Sidney, Edmund Spenser, and Christopher Marlowe). It was also an era of military glory, especially the defeat of the huge Spanish Armada in 1588.

Globe—the Globe Theater housed Shakespeare's acting company, the Lord Chamberlain's Men (later known as the King's Men). Built in 1598, it caught fire and burned down during a performance of *Henry VIII* in 1613.

hyperbole—an excessively elaborate exaggeration used to create special emphasis or a comic effect, as in Montague's remark that his son Romeo's sighs are "adding to clouds more clouds" in *Romeo and Juliet*.

irony—a discrepancy between what a character says and what he or she truly believes, what is expected to happen and what really happens, or what a character says and what others understand.

metaphor—a figure of speech in which one thing is identified with another, such as when Hamlet calls his father a "fair mountain." (See also **simile.**)

monologue—a speech delivered by a single character.

motif—a recurrent theme or image, such as disease in *Hamlet* or moonlight in *A Midsummer Night's Dream*.

oxymoron—a phrase that combines two contradictory terms, as in the phrase "sounds of silence" or Hamlet's remark, "I must be cruel only to be kind."

personification—imparting personality to something impersonal ("the sky wept"); giving human qualities to an idea or an inanimate object, as in the saying "love is blind."

pun—a playful treatment of words that sound alike, or are exactly the same, but have different meanings. In *Romeo and Juliet* Mercutio says, after being fatally wounded, "Ask for me tomorrow and you shall find me a grave man." *Grave* could mean either "a place of burial" or "serious."

simile—a figure of speech in which one thing is compared to another, usually using the word *like* or *as*. (See also **metaphor.**)

soliloquy—a speech delivered by a single character, addressed to the audience. The most famous are those of Hamlet, but Shakespeare uses this device frequently to tell us his characters' inner thoughts.

symbol—a visible thing that stands for an invisible quality, as poison in *Hamlet* stands for evil and treachery.

syntax—sentence structure or grammar. Shakespeare displays amazing variety of syntax, from the sweet simplicity of his songs to the clotted fury of his great tragic heroes, who can be very difficult to understand at a first hearing. These effects are deliberate; if we are confused, it is because Shakespeare means to confuse us.

theme—the abstract subject or message of a work of art, such as revenge in *Hamlet* or overweening ambition in *Macbeth*.

tone—the style or approach of a work of art. The tone of *A Midsummer Night's Dream*, set by the lovers, Bottom's crew, and the fairies, is light and sweet. The tone of *Macbeth*, set by the witches, is dark and sinister.

tragedy—a story that traces a character's fall from power, sanity, or privilege. Shakespeare's well-known tragedies include *Hamlet*, *Macbeth*, and *Othello*.

tragicomedy—a story that combines elements of both tragedy and comedy, moving a heavy plot through twists and turns to a happy ending.

verisimilitude—having the appearance of being real or true.

understatement—a statement expressing less than intended, often with an ironic or comic intention; the opposite of hyperbole.

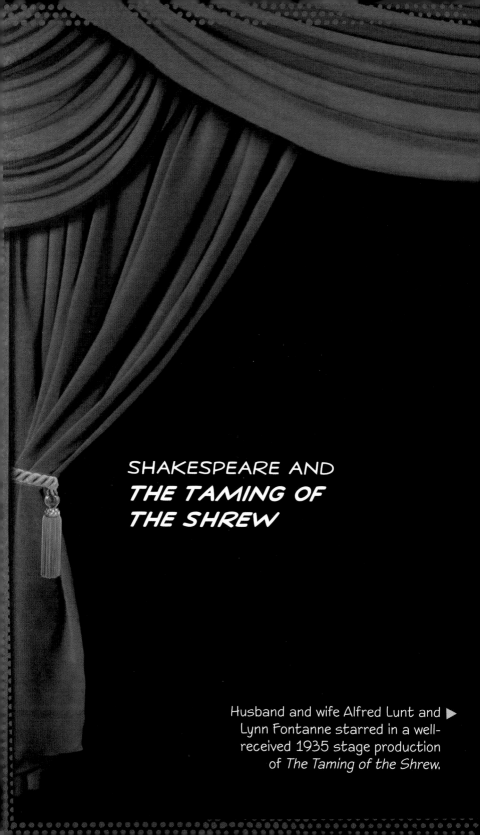

SHAKESPEARE AND
THE TAMING OF THE SHREW

Husband and wife Alfred Lunt and ▶
Lynn Fontanne starred in a well-
received 1935 stage production
of *The Taming of the Shrew*.

Shakespeare and The Taming of the Shrew

CHAPTER ONE

THE TAMING OF THE SHREW IS ONE OF SHAKESPEARE'S EARLIEST COMEDIES; IT WAS PROBABLY WRITTEN IN THE MID-1590S, ALTHOUGH THE EXACT YEAR IS UNCERTAIN. THE MAIN PLOT CONCERNS THE RELATIONSHIP AND MARRIAGE OF KATHERINE (KATE) MINOLA, WHO HAS A DIFFICULT PERSONALITY (TO SAY THE LEAST), AND PETRUCHIO, A BRASH YOUNG MAN OF VERONA WHO IS DETERMINED TO TAME HER. THE SUBPLOT COVERS THE MORE ROMANTIC AND CONVENTIONAL COURTING OF BIANCA, KATE'S YOUNGER SISTER.

An acting troupe called the Queen's Men may have been the first to perform this Shakespeare play. The Queen's Men was formed in 1583 at the command of Elizabeth I. It was one of two dominant acting companies of the period. The other company, for which Shakespeare worked as an actor and playwright, was the Lord Chamberlain's Men, founded in 1594. The Queen's Men was renamed the King's Men in 1603 when King James took the throne. These companies performed at court primarily in the winter and toured the British countryside in the summer.

The Taming of the Shrew is a farce, a dramatic work whose aim is making the audience laugh. In a farce, the comedy is usually exaggerated to the point of ridiculousness; a typical farce is full of slapstick and bawdy humor. Theatrical farce, which often satirizes social customs, has been popular since ancient Greek and Roman times. *The Taming of the Shrew* certainly contains all these elements: the play is full of puns and off-color jokes and often moves at a frantic pace toward the happy ending.

Shakespeare's other farcical plays are *The Comedy of Errors* (written between 1592 and 1594) and *The Merry Wives of Windsor* (probably written in 1597). *The Comedy of Errors* deals with two sets of identical twins separated at birth. When they all meet, wild mishaps result. *Merry Wives* is Shakespeare's only play that is centered on English middle-class life in the Elizabethan era. It tells of the mix-up when the fat knight Sir John Falstaff, short of cash, arrives in Windsor in search of a wealthy wife. When he sends identical love letters to two women, neither of whom is interested in him, the fun begins.

In a farce, there is generally not much character development; the play usually rests on its comic situations and loud humor. In *The Taming of the Shrew*, however, Kate and Petruchio are more than merely stock players. Kate exhibits shrewish ways, but the audience quickly senses that her younger sister, Bianca, may be an understandable cause for her prickly personality. Even Kate's father's preference for her sister is obvious.

When reading this play, one should keep in mind the status of women in general and the societal expectation that most women would marry. Women in general were expected to abide by the wishes of men, first their fathers and then their husbands. A woman's education began in the home. Upper-class girls might get a classical education like their brothers did, since it was thought that such an education would help to attract a desirable suitor.

In general, an Elizabethan woman could not go to a university or become a doctor or vote or act in the theater or inherit money from her father, except in the case of royalty. In short, unless a woman entered a religious order, her only other option was marriage. Of course, as in all other societies, there were some women who never married. As a rule, a married woman was expected to subordinate herself to her husband or sometimes to a senior male relative.

Applying discipline to make a young girl or a headstrong wife behave is not a new theme in literature, especially in Elizabethan times, when it was accepted that a woman's duty was to submit to her husband. Bucking a widely accepted and unquestioned tradition is part of what made *The Taming of the Shrew* and similar comedies so amusing.

To challenge such a time-honored custom was unheard of. In some cases, applying discipline might include physical violence. Kate is not subjected to physical violence. However, the play does imply that physically or emotionally dominating one's wife is desirable—even if the process is often amusing. Still, the play has been called sexist and even misogynistic (hateful to women). Some have called it cruel. Even today, scholars argue over Shakespeare's extent of meaning. Was he making fun of the mores of the times or only exaggerating to point them out? He was, after all, an Elizabethan himself.

Elizabethan audiences generally liked *The Taming of the Shrew*, despite some harsh language and its rough ways. In the seventeenth century this play was one of many Shakespeare plays that were rewritten to tone down the bawdiness; the play decreased in popularity, though it was revived in the eighteenth century. Modern audiences are often divided regarding Kate's treatment; some are amused, and some are offended. As in the original productions, modern directors tend to stress the farcical elements.

AN AMUSED LORD LISTENS TO CHRISTOPHER SLY DURING THE INDUCTION IN A PERFORMANCE BY THE UTAH SHAKESPEARE FESTIVAL.

The Taming of the Shrew is unlike most Elizabethan romantic comedies because it focuses on life after the wedding rather than events leading up to it. Especially among the upper classes, love was generally not a primary consideration in marriage. Of far greater concern was the acquisition of land or money or some kind of social or political power.

The Taming of the Shrew was performed for the first time during the reign of Elizabeth I (1558–1603). Audiences were familiar with the marriage contract, a legal document agreed to by the parents or guardians of the bride and groom. The wedding was in fact a merger, much like business mergers of today. Property and social power were moved within families. The bride's dowry became the property of the groom.

The entire play takes place in Italy, mostly in the city of Padua. A number of Shakespeare's other works also are set in Italy, including *Julius Caesar*, *Two Gentlemen of Verona*, *The Merchant of Venice*, and *Romeo and Juliet*. Despite his fondness for writing plays with Italian settings, there is no evidence that Shakespeare ever traveled to Italy. In fact, there is no evidence that he ever left Great Britain.

Shakespeare opens *The Taming of the Shrew* with a theatrical device called an induction, which is a scene that is related to the play but that stands apart from the main action. A character or characters not involved in the play's central action appear in the induction. (In contrast, a prologue is a speech that is addressed to the audience by a character in the main action of the play.) Although an induction was quite common in sixteenth- and seventeenth-century productions, *The Taming of the Shrew* is the only one of Shakespeare's plays that begins in such a way.

In this comedy, the induction introduces Christopher Sly, part-time tinker and part-time drunk. A nobleman passes and decides to play a trick on the sleeping Sly. When Sly wakes up in the lord's manor, he is told that he is really a nobleman. He is also invited to a performance by a group of traveling players. The action that follows in Padua begins here.

Shakespeare frequently contrasts appearance and reality in *The Taming of the Shrew*. Several characters disguise themselves to hide their true identity; in one instance, a servant impersonates his master. Some directors have treated the main action as an illusion. They have Sly the tinker fall asleep and dream the whole thing. When directors choose this interpretation, they often conclude the play with a scene that shows Sly waking up.

THE PLAY'S THE THING

- OVERVIEW AND ANALYSIS

- LIST OF CHARACTERS

- ANALYSIS OF MAJOR CHARACTERS

Elizabeth Taylor played Kate ▶ opposite Richard Burton as Petruchio in the 1967 film version of *The Taming of the Shrew*.

CHAPTER
TWO

The Play's the Thing

INDUCTION, SCENE 1

OVERVIEW

A tinker, Christopher Sly, is tossed out of an alehouse for refusing to pay for the mugs he has broken. The drunken Sly lies down outside and promptly falls asleep. A lord, returning from a hunting trip, spies the sleeping tinker and decides to make sport of him. The lord's men carry Sly back to the manor, where he is richly dressed and—still in a stupor—put to bed in the best room. The joke will begin when the tinker wakes. He will be told that he is a nobleman who has just revived after a long illness during which he lost his memory. Everyone agrees that this will be an excellent jest.

Before Sly wakes up, a group of traveling players arrives and offers to perform for the lord. The lord agrees to a performance that evening.

However, he tells the players that in the audience will be another lord who has never before seen a play. They must promise not to laugh if he exhibits any strange behavior.

The lord also sends instructions to Bartholomew, his page boy. The young man is to dress in women's clothes and play the part of Sly's wife, who will be overjoyed that her husband has recovered his sanity. The lord even has a plan if Bartholomew cannot cry on cue: "An onion will do well for such a shift, / Which in a napkin being close convey'd / Shall in despite enforce a watery eye." Thus the grand jest is about to begin.

ANALYSIS

To convince a sleeping character that, upon waking, he is someone else is not new in literature. In this case, the personality of the sleeper—Christopher Sly—is quickly established. He is a clown to be sure and not of good repute, but he is also a proud man and convinced of his own worth. When he is called a rogue by the hostess of the alehouse, he quickly denies the accusation: "The Slys are no rogues; look in the chronicles; we came in with Richard Conqueror." He means William the Conqueror, who invaded England in 1066 to take the English crown.

The lord's plan to convince a beggar like Sly that he is indeed a nobleman would have been appreciated by Elizabethan audiences. There was a significant difference between nobility and peasants in Elizabethan society, so seeing a poor tinker masquerade as a lord would have amused contemporary audiences.

Most interesting in this scene is a glimpse into how most men of that time regarded women. A woman was expected to tend to the needs and wants of a man, and the man, in return, provided for her and protected her. The lord sends instructions to his servant Bartholomew on how to act as Sly's wife:

The lord instructs his servant to be so overly emotive that he will be a caricature of the archetypal helpless and devoted wife.

INDUCTION, SCENE 2

OVERVIEW

A bewildered Sly wakes to find himself in a richly decorated bedchamber and immediately wants a drink. The servants and the lord himself, who is dressed as a servant, tell Sly that he has been out of his mind for the past fifteen years. Sly is understandably skeptical, but they are insistent in their joy over his recovery.

When Bartholomew enters dressed as his wife, Sly is a bit more willing to be convinced. However, after inviting the disguised page to join him in bed, he is told that he is not yet fully recovered. Instead, he will now be entertained with a comic performance. In this manner, the story of the taming of a shrew begins.

ANALYSIS

In this lively and amusing scene, Sly shows himself to be a person not easily swayed. He insists he is a peddler when the servants address him as a lord. He even scoffs at the idea of delicacies and riches that are offered to him. However, it is quite understandable that, in the end, he allows himself to agree to the deception; what poor tinker—or poor anyone—would not like to wake up rich? At the outset, when Sly believes himself to be a tinker, he speaks in prose, as do virtually all of Shakespeare's nonnoble characters. When he begins to believe he is a lord, he speaks in poetry but reverts to prose when he wants to take his "wife" to bed. The page in disguise as a woman was quite amusing to Elizabethan audiences since, at the time, female parts were generally played by young boys.

Also of note are the lines with which Shakespeare closes the scene. Despite his lack of education, Sly extends an elegant invitation to his wife: "Come, madam wife, sit by my side and let the world slip; we shall ne'er be younger."

As the scene ends, the main action of the play is about to begin. The story of Sly, except for a mention in Act I, Scene I, is gone. Partly for that reason, *The Taming of the Shrew* is sometimes performed without the Induction. However, the Induction does introduce three important themes of the play: disguise, deceit, and trickery.

ACT I, SCENE 1

OVERVIEW

A wealthy young man named Lucentio arrives in Padua with his servant, Tranio. Lucentio has come to study at one of Italy's universities. Tranio, however, advises him against working too hard: "No profit grows where is no pleasure ta'en." Lucentio agrees: "Tranio, well dost thou advise."

Their conversation is interrupted by a noisy group. Baptista Minola appears with his daughters, Katherine and Bianca, as well as Bianca's two suitors, Gremio and Hortensio. Baptista loudly tells the two men that they cannot court Bianca because her older sister, Katherine, is not yet wed. He does give them permission to court Katherine. However, neither man is interested in the loud and argumentative Katherine. Says Hortensio, "From all such devils, good Lord deliver us!" Katherine in turn threatens the two suitors with violence. After Baptista and his daughters leave, the two men

A CHAGRINED BAPTISTA LOOKS ON AS HORTENSIO TRIES TO SUBDUE THE FEISTY KATE AS SHE GOES AFTER GREMIO IN THE ROYAL SHAKESPEARE COMPANY'S 2008 PRODUCTION.

agree that their only hope for marriage with Bianca is to find someone to marry Katherine.

Hortensio says, "Why, man, there be good fellow sin the world ... would take her with all her faults, and money enough." Gremio replies, "I cannot tell; but I had as lief take her dowry with this condition, to be whipped at the high cross every morning." They are not optimistic as they depart.

In the meantime, Lucentio has fallen in love with Bianca: "Tranio, I burn, I pine, I perish." Lucentio has a plan. Since he cannot court Bianca in public because of Katherine, he will do so in secret. During the loud conversation, he overheard mention of the need of a tutor for Bianca. (Baptista said to his daughter's suitors, "Schoolmasters will I keep within my house, / Fit to instruct her youth.") Lucentio now plans to become that tutor and win her heart with this disguise.

Meanwhile, Tranio will take on the guise of Lucentio and study at the university. The exchange of clothes startles and confuses Lucentio's other servant, Biondello, when he arrives. The servant is told that the masquerade is necessary because Lucentio has killed a man and wearing Tranio's clothes will save his life. Biondello is still confused but does not question the masquerade.

At this point, Sly, in his last appearance in the play, is asked how he likes the play the traveling actors are performing. He declares it to be excellent and cozies up to his wife.

ANALYSIS

Katherine is introduced in this scene as a woman who is sharp-tongued, biting, and hot-tempered. Men instantly dislike her. Gremio remarks, "Though her father be very rich, any man is so very a fool to be married to hell?" Tranio calls her "curst and shrewd." In Elizabethan times, men expected a wife to be submissive to her husband; a hot-headed and cruel woman such as Katherine would not have been looked at as a desirable marriage choice.

"IS IT FOR HIM YOU DO ENVY ME SO?"

Can Katherine's bad behavior be understood in light of the treatment that she has received? She clearly has been less favored than her sister. In this scene she is openly humiliated by her father. In public, Baptista loudly tells Bianca's suitors that Katherine has to get married first and then offers the older daughter to one of them: "If either of you both love Katharina, . . . / Leave shall you have to court her at your pleasure." Who would not be embarrassed—and even cranky and spiteful—at such treatment? Baptista compounds this thoughtless behavior when he goes off to talk to Bianca alone and leaves Katherine to bristle with humiliation: "Why, and I trust I may go too, may I not? What, shall I be appointed hours; as though, belike, I knew not what to take, and what to leave, ha?"

Perhaps under such circumstances, it is possible to view Katherine as independent, clever, proud, and embarrassed rather than shrewish. To be sure, however, it must be admitted that she indeed appears shrewish to the men with whom she comes in contact.

In contrast, Bianca seems to have all the attributes so desired of Elizabethan women; she is angelic, fair, pure, and passive. She is obviously her father's favorite and is used to the adoring attention of men.

To modern audiences, the idea that Lucentio falls in love with Bianca within a few minutes may be a little surprising. However, love at first sight was quite common in the literature of the time and certainly in Shakespeare's plays. In addition, although Lucentio appears to be a sincere lover, his feelings for Bianca may also be perceived as lacking depth. Rather than burning with love, he seems to view her as a prize to be won: "I perish, Tranio, if I achieve not this young modest girl."

This scene introduces the theme of disguise, which becomes so important to the development of the play. In his last appearance at the end of the scene, an apparently impatient Sly says these words to his supposed wife: "'Tis a very excellent piece of work, madam lady: would 'twere done!"

OVERVIEW

Enter Petruchio, a brash young man from Verona, who has come to Padua to seek his fortune. With his servant, Grumio, he stops at the home of his old friend Hortensio. After some comic misunderstanding between

DOUGLAS FAIRBANKS PLAYED PETRUCHIO IN THE 1929 BLACK-AND-WHITE FILM THE TAMING OF THE SHREW.

Petruchio and his servant, which results in a near brawl, Hortensio appears. He asks the young man why he is in Padua. Petruchio replies that after the death of his father he decided to journey in search of fortune and a wife: "Haply to wive and thrive as best I may." Petruchio hopes to find a rich wife.

This news excites Hortensio, who—friend or not—sees an opportunity to marry off Katherine to Petruchio and win Bianca for himself. However, he does warn Petruchio about Katherine: "She is intolerable curst / And shrewd and froward, so beyond all measure / That, were any state far worse than it is / I would not wed her for a mine of gold."

Petruchio declares that he is not choosy: "Hortensio, peace! Thou know'st not gold's effect: / Tell me her father's name and 'tis enough." He does not care how the woman behaves as long as she has a rich father. To get on with the courtship, he decides he must see her that very day. He asks Hortensio to go with him to her father's home. Hortensio agrees, but since he is forbidden to court Bianca, he disguises himself as a tutor for her.

Lucentio arrives, also disguised as a tutor, Cambio. He is with Gremio. Unaware of Cambio's feelings, Gremio has agreed to introduce him to Baptista. He thinks that Cambio will sing Gremio's praises to Bianca's father. At this point, Hortensio gives Gremio the good news that Petruchio intends to become Katherine's suitor. Although Gremio is skeptical and wants to know if Hortensio has outlined Katherine's faults to him, Petruchio declares that nothing will stand in the way of his winning her.

ANALYSIS

Petruchio makes his first appearance in this scene. It is obvious that he is brash, self-confident, and has a quick mind, which he will need in his encounters with Katherine. He also has a quick temper, which sometimes results in physical violence. It is quite easy at first glance to judge Petruchio

FOR I AM HE AM BORN TO TAME YOU, KATE.

as a mere fortune hunter, as he is willing to marry Katherine practically sight unseen for her money.

But it should be remembered that in Elizabethan England and later, marriage was very often a way in which to ensure one's fortune or well being. Petruchio has already inherited the family estate following his father's death, but he sees an opportunity to significantly—and easily—increase his wealth through marriage. "I come to wive it wealthily in Padua; / If wealthily, then happily in Padua," he proclaims. Also, from the initial view of his character, it is easy to believe that Petruchio perhaps regards marriage with the ill-tempered Kate as a challenge. With the introduction of Petruchio, the audience knows that the relationship between the two protagonists will be off to a rocky start.

Gremio appears again and comes off as a bit of a fool. He thinks he can use Cambio (disguised Lucentio) to help him win Bianca, never realizing that Cambio is after Bianca for himself. With Lucentio and Hortensio disguised as tutors and Tranio disguised as Lucentio, the use of disguise becomes more widespread in this scene.

ACT II, SCENE 1

OVERVIEW

All is madness as the scene opens at the home of Baptista Minola. Katherine, in a fury, has literally tied Bianca's hands and is demanding to know which of the two suitors the younger woman favors. Bianca replies, "Believe me, sister, of all the men alive / I never yet beheld that special face; / Which

I could fancy more than any other." Katherine does not believe her, and when Bianca asks if Katherine envies her, Katherine hits her sister. Baptista enters and tries to stop the fighting. The fact that he pities Bianca and scolds Kate only angers Katherine the more: "Nay, now I see / She is your treasure." Claiming that her father's favoritism will doom her to being unwed, she stomps off. Baptista moans, "Was ever gentleman thus grieved as I?"

Now enter six characters who bring deception to a fine art: Petruchio, who will plead his case for Katherine on a false basis; Hortensio, who is dressed as a tutor named Litio; Lucentio, who is dressed as a tutor named Cambio; Gremio, who is unaware that Lucentio likes Bianca; Tranio, who is dressed as Lucentio; and finally, Biondello, Lucentio's servant.

Almost immediately, Petruchio declares his intention to marry Katherine. Baptista, who of course would like nothing better than to marry off his older daughter, is not so sure: "But for my daughter, Katherine, this I know, / She is not for your turn, the more my grief." Petruchio quickly offers Baptista the disguised Hortensio as a music instructor for the two young women. Baptista is about to question Petruchio's sanity in wooing Katherine when he is interrupted by Gremio, who has noted how quickly the tutor has been accepted. In turn, Gremio presents his own tutor, Cambio, the disguised Lucentio. Baptista accepts: "A thousand thanks, Signior Gremio. Welcome, good Cambio." Not to be outdone, Tranio now chimes in. Disguised as his master, Lucentio, he offers gifts in exchange for being allowed to woo Bianca. Baptista welcomes him, too.

The two phony tutors leave. Baptista and Petruchio discuss Katherine's dowry, and Baptista warns the confident Petruchio that Katherine will not be easy to woo. They are soon interrupted by Hortensio, who is wearing a lute around his neck, thanks to Katherine. He explains what happened during her music lesson: "When, with a most impatient devilish spirit, /

'Frets, call you these?' quote she; 'I'll fume with them:' / And, with that word, she struck me on the head."

Petruchio is not upset by what he hears and claims he is ready to be married. Exit Hortensio and Baptista and enter Katherine, whom Petruchio immediately calls Kate. He begins to tell her how lovely she is, but Kate is having none of it. The banter continues until she gets annoyed and hits him. Petruchio responds, "I swear I'll cuff you, if you strike again." Kate, who remains feisty despite his threat, threatens him in turn: "So may you lose your arms; / If you strike me, you are no gentleman; / And if no gentleman, why then no arms."

The verbal jousting goes on until Baptista, Gremio, and Tranio return. Petruchio shocks them by announcing the wedding will be on Sunday. Kate makes her feelings clear: "I'll see thee hang'd on Sunday first." Petruchio then shocks Kate when he announces to the others that she is actually a very loving, gentle woman and is only putting on an act of being gruff and argumentative before others: "I tell you, 'tis incredible to believe / How much she loves me: O, the kindest Kate! / She hung about my neck; and kiss on kiss / She vied so fast, protesting oath on oath." Kate is strangely silent at this point. Petruchio says, "We will have rings and things and fine array; / And kiss me, Kate, we will be married o' Sunday." Kate says nothing, and she and Petruchio leave.

Baptista, Gremio, and Tranio are left alone in shock as they suddenly realize that Bianca is now available for marriage to the highest bidder. Tranio, disguised as Lucentio, simply outbids Gremio. The wedding is set for the Sunday following Kate's marriage. There is one small problem, however. Baptista wants to meet Lucentio's father (Vincentio) to make sure that the dowry will be as promised. Otherwise, Bianca will marry Gremio. The two men leave, and Tranio is left to figure out who he can get to impersonate Lucentio's father.

This scene, which is the longest in the play and the only scene in the entire act, advances the action and more fully explains the motives of the characters. First, the audience gains a better understanding of Kate. Her physical and verbal attack on Bianca at the beginning of the scene is likely due to the fact that the younger woman has many suitors and Kate has none. When their father enters, it is again obvious which daughter he favors. Kate responds, "What, will you not suffer me? Nay now I see / She is your treasure, she must have a husband; / I must dance bare-foot on her wedding day." Her father's frustration in turn causes her to lash out at him; his frustration increases further. It is a never-ending cycle.

The character of Baptista is fleshed out in this scene. In most ways he acts as a loving father to Kate, as when he declares to Petruchio that the most important thing is for the young man to earn her love: "Ay, when the special thing is well obtain'd, / That is, her love; for that is all in all." Yet in the end he accepts the offered wedding arrangement even when Kate says no: "I know not what to say; but give me your hands; / God send you joy, Petruchio! 'tis a match." Although he is eager to see his younger daughter married, he wants to ensure her financial security— and to some extent, his own. As he says to Tranio, who is impersonating his master, Lucentio, "I must confess your offer is the best; / And, let your father make her the assurance, / She is your own; else, you must pardon me, / If you should die before him, where's her dower?" In other words, Baptista wants to make sure that whatever happens to Lucentio, money will be forthcoming to Bianca so that he (Baptista) will not be obliged to support her.

In this scene the battle begins between Petruchio and Kate. It is obvious from the outset that, unlike any other man Kate has known, he has the wits and the will to stand up to her. So it is possible that even though she verbally assaults him as she does all others, she may accept him as an equal. Kate is content with her shrewish ways; with them she either gets what she wants or is left alone. However, Petruchio stands up to her every verbal joust and delivers his own just as strongly. Though she would not admit it, Kate is intrigued by, if not attracted to, this new behavior. Otherwise, why does she remain remarkably silent when Petruchio announces their wedding date at the end of the scene?

Petruchio is a man of considerable wit and patience. He can and does stand up to anything Kate can toss at him, and in fact, there is even an indication that he actually likes her spirited nature. After Hortensio tells of Kate's bashing him in the head with the lute, Petruchio replies, "Now, by the world, it is a lusty wench; / I love her ten times more than e'er I did." Petruchio makes no effort to hide the fact that he wants to marry for money, but it also seems that Kate is a challenge he is eager to face— and conquer.

In this scene, the marriage dates for both daughters are set, and the suitors' disguises and deceptions proceed. The bidding for Bianca between Gremio and Tranio at the end of the scene makes fun of the manner in which many marriages were arranged in Elizabethan times. It is much like an auction, with the bride going to the highest bidder. In this case, of course, it is more amusing because Tranio, disguised as his master, merrily promises dowry money that is not his.

SHE BIDS
YOU COME
TO HER.

IN THIS SCENE FROM A PRODUCTION BY THE UTAH SHAKESPEARE FESTIVAL, BIANCA SITS WITH HER LATIN TUTOR, WHO IS ACTUALLY LUCENTIO IN DISGUISE.

ACT III, SCENE 1

OVERVIEW

It is the Saturday before Kate's wedding. Lucentio and Hortensio, in their disguises as tutors, are alone with Bianca. They argue over which one should instruct her first—without the other present. Bianca solves the problem by telling Hortensio to go away and tune his instrument while Lucentio gives her a language lesson.

Lucentio indicates his feelings for Bianca in the passage that she must translate from Latin. She turns him away gently: "In time I may believe, yet I mistrust." After several attempts to break in, Hortensio finally manages to start Bianca's music lesson. In much the same way as Lucentio had done, Hortensio tries to get his message of love across during his lesson with Bianca, and so he writes it in a music scale, but Bianca is not so gentle in rebuking this second suitor. In fact, in a flirtatious way she is actually being devious since she is now aware of Lucentio's disguise.

Bianca is called away by a messenger. At this point, Hortensio begins to realize that Lucentio is really in love with Bianca. He then ponders Bianca's "wandering" and "ranging" affections. If she is inconstant as he suspects, Hortensio says he will find another woman right away.

ANALYSIS

In this brief, humorous scene, the two suitors for Bianca's hand demonstrate their petty jealousies; in turn, Bianca is shown as something other than a demure, dutiful young woman. The suitors are so determined to outdo each other that they cannot even come to an agreement on who will give the first lesson. Bianca steps in and decides which one will be first: "I'll not be tied to hours nor 'pointed times, / But learn my lessons as I please myself. / And, to cut off all strife, here sit we down; / Take you [Hortensio] your instrument, play you the whiles; / His [Lucentio's] lecture will be done ere you have tuned."

Although both men are clever in their long and rather ridiculous explanations of Latin translations and music scales, it is quickly evident whom Bianca prefers. She does not, of course, really love Lucentio, but she makes it quite clear that she prefers him to Hortensio.

ACT III, SCENE 2

It is Kate's wedding day, and everyone has gathered except the groom. Deciding she has been left at the altar, Kate exits weeping. Biondello arrives to tell everyone that Petruchio is on his way, but he is wearing strange clothes: "a new hat and an old jerkin, a pair of old breeches thrice turned, a pair of boots that have been candle-cases . . . an old rusty sword ta'en out of the town armoury with a broken hilt." In addition, he is riding an old horse. Petruchio arrives thus attired and will not change his clothes. He declares that Kate is marrying him, not his attire: "To me she's married, not unto my clothes."

While Petruchio goes off to find Kate, Tranio and Lucentio stay behind to discuss how they are going to find an impersonator for Lucentio's father. Now Gremio enters; he has come from the church, where there was much commotion. At the ceremony, Petruchio swore so loudly that the priest dropped his book and Petruchio hit him.

After loudly kissing Kate in front of the startled onlookers, Petruchio declared that he and Kate were going to their home in the country and would not stay for the wedding dinner. Kate protested, but Petruchio drew his sword. The couple left behind a rather shocked group of wedding guests. Has tempestuous Kate met her match?

ANALYSIS

In this scene, the audience hears about what is certainly one of the most farcical weddings to be found in all of drama. The scene also launches Petruchio's plan to change the personality of his new wife. He will do so by acting as she acts—loudly and rudely. In other words, he will parade his nasty personality in front of her to make her realize what she seems like to others. However, Petruchio will also show that he cherishes her, and he will treat her like a damsel in distress at the end of the scene. He will, in effect, kill her with kindness.

At the outset, the audience senses trouble ahead when the groom is late for the wedding. Both Baptista and Kate are well aware of the consequences if he does not show up. Baptista is worried about what people will say: "And yet we hear not of our son-in-law, / What will be said? What mockery will it be, / To want the bridegroom when the priest attends / To speak the ceremonial rites of marriage!"

Kate does not want to hear about her father's humiliation; she is concerned for her own: "No shame but mine: I must, forsooth, be forced / To give my hand opposed against my heart / Unto a mad-brain rudesby full of spleen." In other words, it is bad enough that she is forced to marry someone she does not love or even know, but he is a rude man ("rudesby") and insincere besides.

Petruchio does arrive, though, wearing an outlandish costume and behaving boorishly. To add further insult, note that Baptista, as in an earlier scene, is concerned only with his own problem of getting rid of Kate. Instead of being insulted for his daughter by Petruchio's lateness and ridiculous attire, Baptista comments, "I'm glad he's come, howsoe'er he comes." It does not matter that his lateness and the way he is dressed are offensive to Kate; it matters only that the wedding will go on.

Petruchio continues acting boorishly by smacking the priest at the ceremony. This behavior is meant to be a lesson for Kate, since she has already struck a few people, including Petruchio, by this time. When

"WHY THIS IS FLAT KNAVERY."

Kate argues with Petruchio about skipping the wedding feast, he takes her away by force. However, Petruchio's intention to teach Kate a lesson through his behavior is so far lost on her. She apparently does not recognize herself in his actions. Interestingly, both characters use ill-temper for a purpose. Kate uses hers to hide her humiliation at her father's treatment of her. Petruchio uses his bad manners to change the bad manners of his wife.

Some Shakespeare scholars question Kate's true feelings for Petruchio at this point. Until this scene, she has resisted all attempts to subdue her or change her ways. Why not simply refuse to go to the church? One answer may be that she has been formally betrothed, and a refusal to go to the church would have ruined her—and her family's—reputation. In addition, might not just the status of marriage and the opportunity to leave her father's home have become a strong pull for the headstrong Kate?

ACT IV, SCENE 1

OVERVIEW

Grumio has been sent ahead to tell the servants at Petruchio's home in Verona that Petruchio and his bride are arriving, but he is not very happy about the trip. "Fie, fie on all tired jades, on all mad masters, and all foul ways! . . . Was ever a man so weary?" He tells another servant, Curtis, about the disastrous journey from Padua with the newlyweds fighting all the way. At one point, Kate's horse tripped and she fell into the mud, and Petruchio left her there.

Petruchio's ill treatment of Kate continues at his home. When the couple arrives, Petruchio loudly criticizes Grumio for not having anyone on hand to meet them. Then he demands dinner—and quickly. When it arrives, he does not like anything, declares that the mutton is burned, and ends up throwing it at the servants. By this time, Kate is starving and anxious to eat:

NEITHER PETRUCHIO (RICHARD BURTON)
NOR KATE (ELIZABETH TAYLOR) LOOK
EXCITED TO GET MARRIED IN THIS SCENE
FROM THE 1967 MOVIE.

"I pray you, husband, be not so disquiet; / The meat was well, if you were so contented."

Petruchio is having none of her pleas, and so they head off to the bed chamber. At scene's end, Petruchio returns, and now his plan becomes obvious to the audience. He compares Kate to a wild falcon that must be trained to obey: "And thus I'll curb her mad and headstrong humour, / He that knows better how to tame a shrew, / Now let him speak; 'tis charity to show."

ANALYSIS

This scene is especially interesting for two reasons. Coupled with the wedding fiasco, it presents Petruchio in a most unlikeable light because of rude behavior toward everyone, no matter the reason. When Grumio tells Curtis of Petruchio's conduct on the journey from the wedding, Curtis remarks, "By this reckoning he is more shrew than she." The scene also shows Kate beginning to change, as when she tries to stop Petruchio from beating his servant: "Patience, I pray you; 'twas a fault unwilling." Kate is starting to put someone else's welfare before her own.

Audiences found Grumio's descriptions of the journey to Petruchio's country home amusing. The journey itself is not part of the play, probably because it would have been difficult to stage, especially the incident when Kate's horse dumps her in the mud. However, Grumio's report causes a good deal of laughter, especially when he talks about his exasperation at having to travel with the newlyweds. Note also Petruchio's tactics; instead of helping Kate when her horse falls, he yells at Grumio for letting it happen.

The rest of the scene highlights Petruchio's methods of taming his wife. As Kate stands by helpless, tired, and hungry, he screams at the servants and dumps their dinner on the floor. He claims that nothing is good enough for his wife. Kate reacts much as Petruchio wants her to and decidedly against her character. She finds nothing wrong with the food or the servants. In fact, the few lines she speaks implore Petruchio to be patient and calm.

Most critics read Petruchio's actions at this point as role playing. He wants to show Kate how her own behavior is viewed by others. To do so, he acts in a way more boorish than she ever did. As a result the audience begins to see Kate much more sympathetically. She was subject to a father's disinterest only to be ruled now by a husband who humiliates her even more. This treatment forces her to look at others in a different light.

Petruchio ends the scene by comparing his tactics with Kate to those of a lord who is taming a falcon. He will deny her food and sleep and act outrageously, all under the guise of wanting only the best for her. "This is a way to kill a wife with kindness," says Petruchio of his plan to rid Kate of her "headstrong" ways.

ACT IV, SCENE 2

OVERVIEW

The scene shifts back to Padua, where the masquerade continues. Hortensio is still smarting from his apparent rejection by Bianca; so he tells Tranio (disguised as Lucentio) of Bianca's seeming interest in Cambio (who is actually Lucentio). Tranio plays along and tells Hortensio that he is no longer interested in Bianca: "I will with you, if you be so contented, / Forswear Bianca and her love for ever." Tranio gets Hortensio to agree: "Here is my hand and here I firmly vow / Never to woo her more, but do forswear her." Tranio has cleverly removed the other competition.

Tranio now tells Bianca and Lucentio that Hortensio has decided, like Petruchio, to marry for money. In fact, Hortensio will visit Petruchio and attend his "taming school" to learn how to handle the situation.

Now Biondello arrives with further news. An old man, a schoolteacher from Mantua, has appeared in town. He will be the perfect person to impersonate Lucentio's father so that Baptista will be convinced of the wedding dowry. They must get the old man to agree to the ruse.

Tranio comes up with a clever plan. He tells the schoolteacher that the dukes of Padua and Mantua are at war. In fact, he tells him, "'Tis death for any one in Mantua / To come to Padua." The gullible old man is quite understandably shocked and scared. Tranio offers him protection; all he has to do is disguise himself as Vincentio of Pisa. Then he will be safe. In return for this protection, the schoolteacher must agree to face Baptista as Lucentio's father and—if asked—confirm the dowry money. Under the circumstances, the schoolteacher agrees.

ANALYSIS

The purpose of this scene is mainly to advance the subplot of the play. Hortensio gives up his quest of Bianca. Bianca's feelings for Lucentio, which have already been revealed to the audience, are confirmed, and the couple's marriage, an important part of Act V, Scene 2, is set up. In addition, Tranio finds an old man to impersonate Lucentio's father and satisfy Baptista about the dowry money.

The audience also learns more about Bianca's suitors Hortensio and Tranio. Hortensio is quite fickle regarding women and marriage. First he says he will marry for beauty but then decides kindness is more important: "Kindness in women, not their beauteous looks, / Shall win my love." However, it seems to be the widow's wealth that makes her most appealing to Hortensio as a prospective wife. So, despite what Hortensio may claim, neither beauty nor kindness nor love are priorities for him. Like Petruchio, Hortensio will marry for money.

In contrast to Hortensio, Tranio shows himself to be a clever and quick-witted fellow. First, he gets Hortensio to scorn Bianca, and then he tricks the schoolteacher into impersonating Lucentio's father. His loyalty to Lucentio is also apparent in this scene, as Tranio uses his flair for deceit and manipulation to win Bianca for his master.

The schoolteacher readily accepts without question Tranio's story that hostilities exist between the dukes of Padua and Mantua. He is so taken in that he considers himself lucky to have Tranio's protection and calls him "the patron of my life and liberty."

With one short line in this scene, Bianca gives an indication that she will be less than obedient when she marries Lucentio. When Tranio declares that Hortensio will tame the widow he marries, Bianca replies, "He says so, Tranio." She means that what he says may not, in fact, be what happens. In fact, in the last scene, the widow defies her new husband, as does Bianca hers.

Tranio also makes an interesting statement in this scene. He says to Bianca that Hortensio "is gone unto the taming-school." Although he does go, in fact, Hortensio says no such thing in his conversation with Tranio. Critics say that Hortensio either was supposed to have delivered that information offstage or else the lines were somehow lost or dropped from the play over the centuries.

ACT IV, SCENE 3

OVERVIEW

Back at Petruchio's home, Kate has been denied food and is starving. She has also been without sleep. In desperation, she tries to get Grumio to bring her food. Instead, he taunts her with thoughts of food. Kate gives him a beating and orders him out.

Enter Petruchio with Hortensio, who has come for the "taming school." Petruchio offers Kate food, but first she must thank him for it. She reluctantly agrees.

Shortly afterward, a tailor arrives. Petruchio has announced that they will wear the finest clothes before making a trip to Baptista's house in Padua. However, Petruchio finds fault with everything the tailor makes, especially the gown that Kate likes. He says,

> THY GOWN? WHY, AY; COME, TAILOR, LET US SEE'T.
> O MERCY, GOD! WHAT MASQUING STUFF IS HERE?
> WHAT'S THIS? A SLEEVE? 'TIS LIKE A DEMI-CANNON;
> WHAT, UP AND DOWN, CARVED LIKE AN APPLE TART?

When Petruchio sends the tailor home with Kate's gown, she exclaims, "I never saw a better-fashion'd gown." Petruchio tells Hortensio to assure the tailor that he will be paid in full the following day.

Petruchio tells Kate they will travel to Padua in their old clothes. Then he says they should leave right away to be in Padua by midday. Kate corrects him; it is, in fact, already almost two in the afternoon, not seven in the morning, as he says. Petruchio begins ranting. He accuses her of contradicting him and calls off the trip. They will not leave until she agrees with whatever time he says it is: "I will not go to-day; and ere I do, It shall be what o'clock I say it is."

ANALYSIS

Although it seems in this scene that Kate is beginning to change as a result of Petruchio's tactics, the change is not real. An extremely hungry Kate begs Grumio to bring her food. Instead, he taunts her, and it is obvious that he enjoys this taunting game: "How say you to a fat tripe finely broil'd?" When she agrees, he says, "I fear 'tis choleric." Then he asks, "Why say you to a piece of beef and mustard?" When she agrees, he says, "Ay but the mustard is too hot a little." Frustrated at being treated as she has treated others for years, Kate reverts to her old ways: "Go, get thee gone, thou false deluding slave." Then she hits him.

When Petruchio finally brings Kate food, she does not thank him, and he threatens to take it away. Kate now realizes that in order to eat, she must consider her provider. The rules of the game played by Petruchio are becoming clear to her. In this exchange, Petruchio is trying to teach Kate to act in a moderate and caring way toward others.

When Petruchio suggests a visit to Baptista's home, Kate is pleased. It is an environment with which she is familiar and one in which she is accustomed to acting in her shrewish ways. Petruchio has another taming lesson in mind, however. He says they must make the visit in the finest of new clothes. He then rants and raves at the poor work of the tailor to the despair of Kate. Once again Petruchio is showing Kate how she, in fact, has always acted. What Kate does not know is that Petruchio is only pretending to be dissatisfied with the tailor's work; he fully intends to pay him. Kate may think her husband has gone quite mad, but at least the audience knows he is not going to cheat the tradesman; he is merely using the situation to teach Kate a lesson about herself. Petruchio's claim that clothes are unimportant shows him at a level of sensibility that sets him apart from the more superficial mercantile world of Padua.

There is no indication yet that Kate gets Petruchio's message, but Hortensio is somewhat astounded by this display and marvels that now Petruchio actually seems to think he can command the sun.

"HE HATH SOME MEANING IN HIS MAD ATTIRE."

ACT IV, SCENE 4

OVERVIEW

Back in Padua, Tranio, still disguised as Lucentio, and the schoolteacher, pretending to be his father, are at the home of Baptista. The real Lucentio, disguised as Cambio, is also there. The schoolteacher declares the dowry is forthcoming. Lucentio goes off to find Bianca, while Tranio, Baptista, and Lucentio's "father" go off to discuss marriage details.

Lucentio returns, and Biondello tells him that now is the time to marry Bianca. Biondello leaves to find a priest, and Lucentio looks for Bianca to tell her they will soon be married.

ANALYSIS

This short scene moves the action along. It also reveals how marriage works in Elizabethan times. Baptista sells his favored daughter, for whom he has genuine affection, to the highest bidder. As it turns out, the joke is actually on him. When he sends Cambio to tell Bianca that she will marry Lucentio, he is actually sending the real Lucentio. The person he believes to be Lucentio (Tranio) and the schoolteacher he thinks is Lucentio's wealthy father are in fact poor people.

The scene also illustrates Shakespeare's use of disguise. In his plays, upper-class characters tend to take someone who seems to be a member of their class at face value. Therefore, the authenticity of Tranio and the schoolteacher are never questioned by Baptista.

ACT IV, SCENE 5

OVERVIEW

On the road to Padua, Petruchio is ruthless in his resolve to get Kate to submit to authority. It is noon, but he says the moon is shining. When Kate protests, he threatens to cancel the trip, so she agrees, at the urging of Hortensio, that the moon is indeed shining. At this point, Kate understands the game. When Petruchio reverses himself and says the sun is now shining, she agrees once more.

Along the road, they meet the real Vincentio, who is traveling to Padua to see his son, Lucentio. Petruchio says of the old man, "Hast thou beheld a fresher gentlewoman?" Kate agrees, and when Petruchio changes his mind and calls him an old man, she agrees with that statement too.

After the banter, they learn Vincentio's identity. Petruchio tells him that his son was about to marry Kate's sister when last they saw them. Vincentio is shocked by the news. As they continue the journey to Padua, Hortensio is left to marvel at the change in Kate; he vows that he will tame the rich widow he wants to marry in the same way.

ANALYSIS

This short scene is of great importance to the development and conclusion of the plot. Kate now fully realizes the game her husband is playing. Perhaps more to the point, she fully realizes her part in it.

Some critics claim this scene shows that Kate is finally tamed and her spirit broken; other critics think Kate has realized that by changing her outward manner, she is able to get what she wants and to live in peace—even perhaps happiness—with her new husband. She no longer lashes out at people. Affecting a smile and a courteous manner, even when she must agree with the outlandish words of Petruchio, she has a new way of living. Their debate about the moon suggests that she is willing to agree with his "lunacy" and, if necessary, say whatever lunatic thing he wants. Has Kate been tamed at this point? Or has she grown from a child who lashed out in anger and humiliation into a mature woman who understands the rules of society and is determined to live by them—for her own benefit?

Petruchio's manner also changes. He no longer needs to starve Kate or keep her from sleeping in order to change her ways. He no longer needs to threaten or strike the servants to prove his point. In short, he becomes a happier man as well. When he meets Vincentio on the journey and discovers his identity, he is gentle and respectful.

Some find this scene particularly cruel and degrading for Kate. Does Petruchio go too far in trying to change the manner of his wife?

When Petruchio insists that Kate agree that the moon is shining and she does, he says, "Nay, then you lie: it is the blessed sun." When Kate also agrees with that statement, the bewildered Hortensio says, "Petruchio, Go thy ways; the field is won."

To further illustrate Kate's complete compliance, when Vincentio appears on the road, Petruchio says he is a fair young maid. Kate has learned her lesson well, and her immediate agreement with what he says implies that she is beginning to have fun with the game. Petruchio responds, "Why, how now, Kate! I hope thou art not mad: / This is a man, old, wrinkled, faded, wither'd." Kate agrees with Petruchio once again. When she passes the test, there is reason to believe that with Kate's new understanding of the rules of marriage—at least of this marriage—harmony and perhaps love will grow. It does seem as though the taming is complete.

The appearance of Vincentio sets in motion the resolution of the play. The masquerade that has been going on to win the hand of Bianca must be revealed and the disguises unveiled.

Hortensio, the onlooker, wants the widow he will marry to undergo a transformation similar to Kate's. However, he does not understand what has happened to cause a change in the relationship between Kate and Petruchio. All he knows is that he wants this miracle to happen to him as well. As the audience will soon see, Hortensio is in for disappointment.

IN 2003 AN ALL-FEMALE CAST PERFORMED THE TAMING OF THE SHREW AT THE GLOBE THEATER IN LONDON, ENGLAND.

ACT V, SCENE 1

OVERVIEW

In Padua once again, Lucentio, no longer in disguise, and Bianca go to the church to be married. Petruchio, Kate, and Vincentio arrive at Lucentio's house. When Vincentio says he is Lucentio's father, he is called a liar by Baptista and the schoolmaster. Biondello arrives and refuses to recognize Vincentio, who beats him. Then Tranio comes and pretends that he does not know Vincentio either. By now, a perplexed Vincentio is convinced that his son has been murdered.

With everyone thoroughly confused, the newlyweds Lucentio and Bianca arrive. Lucentio explains the hoax, saying the deception was necessary because of his true love for Bianca. The real Vincentio placates the distressed Baptista, and both fathers, although still somewhat confused, are pacified and accepting. They all go inside Lucentio's house for the wedding feast.

Petruchio and Kate are left alone, somewhat amazed themselves. Before they go to join the festivities, Petruchio asks for a kiss from Kate. She is reluctant to do so right out in the street. When Petruchio says they will return home, Kate changes her mind. "Nay, I will give thee a kiss: now pray thee, love, stay."

ANALYSIS

Now is the time for the disguises to be revealed and the subplot—the marriage of Bianca and Lucentio—to reach its climax. This is, in farcical tradition, accomplished in a comic fashion. All might be said to end well except, perhaps, for Vincentio, who is a trifle annoyed. He is not so much bothered that someone stole his identity as he is at being threatened with prison by Tranio and then by Baptista.

"THOU MUST BE MARRIED TO NO MAN BUT ME."

When Vincentio arrives in Padua, he is unprepared for the reaction of his son's servants Biondello and Tranio, whom of course he has long known. When he asks if Biondello has forgotten him, the servant replies, "I could not forget you, for I never saw you before in all my life." Tranio's reaction is much the same, and now Baptista chimes in and calls Vincentio a lunatic. No wonder the old man begins to think his son has been murdered. Actually, Biondello and Tranio are only perpetuating the deceit to gain time until Lucentio shows up after secretly marrying Bianca. When the newlyweds do arrive, Lucentio kneels before his bewildered father. Biondello, Tranio, and the schoolteacher flee the scene as quickly as possible, and Lucentio is left to explain everything to Vincentio and Baptista.

Audiences find much merriment in the wild confusion. The two fathers, Baptista and Vincentio—who were both so angry and bewildered a moment ago—are at least pacified, if still a bit confused, by the marriage of their children.

Only Kate and Petruchio are left standing outside of Lucentio's house. Many think that the play could have ended with this scene because it brings the subplot to an end. It also signifies a significant change, not just in Kate but in Petruchio as well.

Kate suggests that they too go inside to share the feast. Petruchio agrees to her suggestion but says he wants a kiss first. Kate refuses at first not because she does not want to kiss him but because she does not want to do so in public. When Petruchio suggests they leave instead, he seems more playful than authoritative. In their first real display of affection, Kate submits to the kiss and also calls him "love." He returns the affection: "Is not this well? Come, my sweet Kate; / Better once than never, for never too late." This is the third kiss between Kate and Petruchio. It may be extorted but it is at least more sweet. It is also confirmation to Petruchio that Kate will obey his requests in public.

ACT V, SCENE 2

OVERVIEW

A banquet is being held at Lucentio's home to celebrate three marriages: his to Bianca, Petruchio's to Kate, and Hortensio's to the wealthy widow. During dinner, conversation gets heated when Petruchio says to Hortensio's wife, "Hortensio is afeard of you."

Kate joins in when she suspects the widow has insulted Petruchio—and her. "Your husband, being troubled with a shrew, / Measures my husband's sorrow by his woe," she says to Kate. In that single statement she calls Kate a shrew and implies that Kate makes Petruchio unhappy so that he can only imagine that every other husband is unhappy. The two women bicker, and their amused husbands bet on who will win. Bianca stops the argument before it escalates, and the three women exit.

The men are left to talk among themselves. Petruchio teases Tranio for failing to win Bianca's hand, and Tranio rebuts by implying that Kate is the dominant partner in her and Petruchio's marriage. Baptista then offers sympathy to Petruchio for having married "The veriest shrew of all," but Petruchio denies it. He suggests a test: Each of the three newly married men will call for his wife. The man whose wife appears most promptly when she is called will prove which man has married the most obedient woman.

The husbands place bets. Biondello is sent to call Bianca for Lucentio, who is sure his wife will appear immediately. Biondello returns with the message that "she is busy and she cannot come." Grumio goes off with a similar request from Hortensio to the widow. Grumio returns with this reply: "She will not come; she bids you come to her."

Kate, however, appears at the request of her husband and says, "What is your will, sir, that you send for me?" The other two wives are brought in. Petruchio then says he dislikes Kate's hat: "Katherine, that cap of yours becomes you not: / Off with that bauble, throw it under-foot." When she does so, everyone is amazed at how obedient she is. Baptista even remarks, "For she is changed, as she had never been."

Petruchio now asks Kate to speak to the other wives: "Katherine, I charge thee, tell these headstrong women / What duty they do owe their lords and husbands." The widow, for one, is having none of it: "Come, come, you're mocking; we will have no telling."

Kate, however, is willing. She now gives the longest speech of the play—and the most controversial. She tells the women present, "And dart not scornful glances from those eyes, / To wound thy lord, thy king, thy governor." Then she speaks of the female nature: "A woman moved is like a fountain troubled, / Muddy, ill-seeming, thick, bereft of beauty." She speaks of a husband and his duties to his wife: "And for thy maintenance commits his body / To painful labour both by sea and land, / To watch the night in storms, the day in cold, / Whilst thou liest warm at home, secure and safe." What does a husband ask in return for protecting and providing

THE MATCH IS MADE, AND ALL IS DONE.

for his wife, she asks. "And craves no other tribute at thy hands, But love, fair looks and true obedience."

What, Kate asks the women, should they give in return to an honorable man? "Too little payment for so great a debt, / Such duty as the subject owes the prince, / Even such a woman oweth to her husband." They are wrong to act in a "peevish, sullen, sour" manner. She calls such a disobedient woman a "rebel" and "graceless traitor."

Kate now chastises the women, saying that a woman's heart should be as soft as her body:

> I AM ASHAMED THAT WOMEN ARE SO SIMPLE
> TO OFFER WAR WHERE THEY SHOULD KNEEL FOR PEACE
> OR SEEK FOR RULE, SUPREMACY AND SWAY,
> WHEN THEY ARE BOUND TO SERVE, LOVE AND OBEY.
> WHY ARE OUR BODIES SOFT AND WEAK AND SMOOTH,
> UNAPT TO TOIL AND TROUBLE IN THE WORLD,
> BUT THAT OUR SOFT CONDITIONS AND OUR HEARTS
> SHOULD WELL AGREE WITH OUR EXTERNAL PARTS?

At the end of her speech, Kate admits that she was once cross and disobedient: "My mind hath been as big as one of yours, / My heart as great, my reason haply more, / To bandy word for word and frown for frown." She goes on to say that she tried to be strong and bullying like a man but has realized that such a manner was not a successful approach to life. "Then vail your stomachs, for it is no boot." In other words, swallow

LOOK WHAT I SPEAK OR DO OR THINK TO DO.

your pride, it is useless. She ends her speech with these words:

> AND PLACE YOUR HANDS BELOW YOUR HUSBAND'S FOOT;
> IN TOKEN OF WHICH DUTY, IF HE PLEASE,
> MY HAND IS READY; MAY IT DO HIM EASE.

Kate enchants all present with how truly she has been tamed. Once again Petruchio says, "Come on and kiss me, Kate." This time, Kate does not object. "Come, Kate, we'll to bed," says Petruchio, and the two leave the wedding feast to go consummate their marriage. The two other newly married men remain in awe of the change that has taken place in Kate.

> HORTENSIO: NOW, GO THY WAYS;
> THOU HAST TAMED A CURST SHREW.
> LUCENTIO: 'TIS A WONDER, BY YOUR
> LEAVE, SHE WILL BE TAMED SO.

Thus ends the comedy called *The Taming of the Shrew*.

ANALYSIS

This scene has been deemed unnecessary by some and degrading to Kate by others. In her long speech, she appears to be completely subservient to her husband. She points out that a husband is "thy lord, thy life, thy keeper, / Thy head, thy sovereign" and that women are "unapt to toil and trouble in the world." However, the scene does provide some interesting probable outcomes in the lives of all those at the feast.

All the men at the banquet believe Petruchio has married the most shrewish of women. Nevertheless, the growing relationship between Petruchio and Kate may indicate that of all the men, Petruchio has the best chance for a truly happy marriage. His suggestion to bet on which woman will respond most quickly when called, though sometimes regarded as insulting to Kate, merely reflects Elizabethan expectations of proper wifely behavior.

Throughout the play, Bianca is portrayed as pure, obedient, and the ideal wife, although there was a hint of her more assertive side in Act III, Scene 1, when she instructs Hortensio to leave while Lucentio gives her a Latin lesson. With the wager set, however, Lucentio calls for her, and suddenly the fair flower is gone. Bianca has a mind of her own and will use it. Is there trouble ahead? Which sister is the shrew?

Hortensio might be the one who faces the most trouble in the future. He thought he was not only snubbing Bianca by marrying the wealthy widow, but gaining financial independence as well. The widow is also no fool. She may have married Hortensio, but she is not about to give up power to her husband. She wants Hortensio to come to her.

A viewer's or reader's reaction to the play as a whole often depends upon his or her reaction to Kate's speech. Has Kate really changed so much that she is telling each of the other women to submit to her husband? Is Kate really sincere? Or is she being sarcastic about the conventions of marriage and subtly suggesting that the relationship between men and women is complex?

Does the future seem to promise a happy marriage for Kate and Petruchio? Has the shrew been tamed? Kate now kisses her husband without protest. The two no longer spend their time bickering. There has indeed been a change of some kind; the question is whether Kate has been tamed or whether she has simply learned how to handle Petruchio.

'TIS A WONDER, BY YOUR LEAVE, SHE WILL BE TAMED SO.

LIST OF CHARACTERS

Katherine (Kate): The sharp-tongued, quick-witted older daughter of Baptista and protagonist of the play

Petruchio: The gentleman from Verona who wishes only to marry a rich woman

Bianca: The soft-spoken, well-liked younger daughter of Baptista

Baptista Minola: A wealthy man of Padua who is desperate to marry off his oldest daughter

Lucentio: A young man from Pisa who poses as a tutor (Cambio) to win Bianca

Gremio: A suitor for Bianca's hand

Hortensio: A suitor to Bianca, who also poses as a tutor (Litio) to win Bianca

Tranio: Lucentio's clever and comical servant who assumes his master's identity

Grumio: A servant to Petruchio

Biondello: A servant to Lucentio

Vincentio: Lucentio's father

Schoolteacher: A tutor who Tranio convinces to impersonate Vincentio

A Widow: The wealthy woman who marries Hortensio

Christopher Sly: A drunken tinker and the principal character in the Induction who is duped into thinking he is a lord

A Lord: The character in the Induction who plays the trick on Sly

Bartholomew: A servant who pretends to be Sly's wife in the Induction

KATHERINE (KATE)

Shortly after Kate appears on stage, the audience gets the message that she is the shrew of the title. Her nature seems obvious not just from her behavior but also from what is said about her. Kate undoubtedly is fiery,

KATE GIVES AN ICY LOOK IN A SCENE FROM A 2007 PRODUCTION AT WILTON'S MUSIC HALL IN LONDON.

rude, and belligerent. Not surprisingly, men just do not like her. The men who meet her liken marriage to Kate to a torment of the damned.

In Act II, Scene 1, the audience is introduced to the character of the shrew. Kate, an intelligent young woman, has suffered rejection by her own father, who clearly prefers his other daughter. She lives in a world where a woman's best prospect for happiness lies almost exclusively in marriage. It is possible that Kate responds to the humiliation of her situation by lashing out—physically and emotionally—at anyone who comes near. Kate is angry at her world; however, it is the world in which she must live, and so she fights it.

Does Kate actually begin to love Petruchio as the play progresses? After all, she has finally met a man who can stand up to her. Although Petruchio sets out to tame her, he is never physically violent with her; he does threaten at one point to slap her—but only after she slaps him. The fact that he is clearly of stronger character than any man Kate has met so far may well be an attraction.

About halfway through the play, the audience glimpses the beginning of Kate's transformation. Does she really change, or has she instead merely learned to play the game according to Petruchio's rules? Why not agree that it is seven o'clock instead of two if she gets what she wants by agreeing?

Kate's seemingly complete submission at the play's end has been debated. Can such a total change of character be possible? Could she have changed that much, and furthermore, why should she? It may be that Kate has found contentment with a man she admires and even loves, and as his wife, she now commands a respect she did not have before. It may be that Kate simply grew up. It may be that the shrew has not changed a bit, except to become wiser.

PETRUCHIO

Petruchio is no less complicated than Kate. His behavior may be explained by the fact that he wants to change his wife, but what are his motives? At the outset, it is apparent that Petruchio is interested in marriage purely for the money. Before he meets Kate, Hortensio warns him, "I would not wed her for a mine of gold." Petruchio, who is not to be swayed by Kate's reputation, replies, "Hortensio, peace! Thou know'st not gold's effect; / Tell me her father's name and 'tis enough." (I.2)

If money is Petruchio's motivation throughout the play and if he truly cares nothing for the woman he is trying to tame, then why waste time in explaining his character? In addition, he gains the rights to Kate and her fortune as soon as he weds her; so he already has the money. It would seem instead that Petruchio wants peace and a quiet life. If Petruchio is not a man of character, then Shakespeare has written a play about a greedy, money-hungry man who deserves no more than fleeting attention.

Is there, perhaps, a deeper level to Petruchio? Could it be that although his initial interest is in Kate's money, he develops true feelings for her? He clearly finds her beautiful: "For, by this light, whereby I see thy beauty— / Thy beauty that doth make me like thee well" (II.1). If that is so, then his actions, outlandish and boorish as they may seem, become more understandable as his way of showing Kate a better way to happiness.

It does seem reasonable that the mercurial Petruchio would be attracted to a woman of fiery spirit. The gentle Bianca, for instance, would probably bore him. If he can see beneath the outward fire of Kate, then he may well realize the reasons for her behavior and may use his taming methods as a way of making them both happy.

At the same time that Petruchio is trying to change the shrewish ways of his wife, he denies to others that she is a shrew. For instance, in Act II,

Scene 1, he says to Baptista, "If she be curst, it is for policy, / For she's not froward, but modest as the dove; / She is not hot, but temperate as the morn." He is not only trying to change her but change what others think of her as well.

Regardless of whether or not one believes Petruchio has feelings for Kate, it is difficult to find him a sympathetic character throughout. He starves his wife and deprives her of sleep; he humiliates her on their wedding day. As Gremio explains it:

> . . . WHEN THE PRIEST SHOULD ASK,
> IF KATHERINE SHOULD BE HIS WIFE,
> 'AY, BY GOGS-WOUNS,' QUOTH HE; AND SWORE SO LOUD,
> THAT, ALL-AMAZED, THE PRIEST LET FALL THE BOOK;
> AND, AS HE STOOD AGAIN TO TAKE IT UP,
> THIS MAD-BRAIN'D BRIDEGROOM TOOK SUCH A CUFF
> THAT DOWN FELL PRIEST AND BOOK AND BOOK AND PRIEST
> 'NOW TAKE THEM UP,' QUOTH HE, 'IF ANY LIST.' (III.2)

If such behavior was done in the hope of a happy future for them both, his actions may be understood, even if not approved. If, however, Petruchio is mainly a man bent on dominating his wife, he is not a figure to be admired.

Most critics agree that Shakespeare intended Petruchio to be a comic figure with a keen sense of humor, understanding, and patience. His actions, outlandish as they may seem, are intended to change Kate's behavior so that their marriage might be a happy one. In fact, at the end of the play, Petruchio indicates the trust he has in his new wife. First he makes a wager that she will come at his bidding, and she does. He also charges Kate to speak at the banquet. Men did not usually let women speak at such affairs in the sixteenth century. Although Petruchio risked embarrassment, his trust is well placed; Kate gives an acceptable speech. When she is finished, he exclaims, "Why, there's a wench. Come on, and kiss me, Kate" (V.2).

ONLOOKERS QUIETLY WATCH AS
PETRUCHIO APPROACHES KATE ON
THEIR WEDDING DAY.

LUCENTIO

Lucentio represents idyllic love. He is lovesick, devoted, and melodramatic, traits that are clearly conveyed when he declares that he will perish if he does not win Bianca: "Tranio, I burn, I pine, I perish" (I.1). When he talks about Bianca, he is poetic, his feelings reminiscent of the love expressed in sonnets. Lucentio even describes Bianca as the idealized fair maiden that is the traditional object of so many sonnets: "I saw her coral lips to move / And with her breath she did perfume the air" (I.1).

Throughout much of the play, Lucentio and Bianca's relationship seems uncomplicated, genuine, and pure, especially in comparison with the rocky relationship between Petruchio and Kate.

The fact that Lucentio's love is unaffected by monetary gain or social considerations differentiates him from the other male characters, particularly Bianca's other suitors. Lucentio's idealism also sets him apart from the pragmatic Petruchio. He perceives Bianca to be the perfect woman, and therefore expects her to be the perfect wife. After they are married, Lucentio even wagers a hundred crowns that Bianca will appear when he beckons. She, of course, does not. Lucentio becomes petty and blames his loss on Bianca's foolishness only to have Bianca point out that he is the fool for having ideal expectations.

BIANCA

Bianca is Baptista's younger daughter. Mild-mannered, sweet, and demure, she is the opposite of Kate. Because of her beauty, charm, and large dowry, Bianca has several suitors.

Despite her maidenly virtues, Bianca seems selfish. In Act II, Scene 1, when Kate leads the bound Bianca and demands to know which suitor Bianca "lov'st best," Bianca declares that she doesn't love any of them. Bianca knows that Kate has no suitors of her own, so her show of indifference toward her many suitors is inconsiderate.

Bianca then asks Kate about Gremio, "Is it for him you do envy me so?" Bianca is aware Kate dislikes her, but she still flaunts her popularity. She also plays the innocent victim, letting her father chastise Kate: "Why dost thou wrong her that did ne'er wrong thee? / When did she cross thee with a bitter word?" (II.1). Is Bianca as blameless as Baptista seems to think?

By the final scene the sisters seem to have reversed their roles. Bianca is no longer quiet and unassuming; instead she is shrewish. She disregards her new husband Lucentio's wishes and insults him for expecting her to be obedient: "The more fool you, for laying on my duty" (V.2). Kate, in contrast, is agreeable.

BAPTISTA

Baptista is presented as a worried father whose main problem is finding a suitable marriage for his older daughter, Kate. At first glance, he garners sympathy for being stuck with a daughter who has the reputation of being a shrew: she is hot-headed, disobedient, and mean. However, sympathy for him soon disappears (at least to modern audiences) as it becomes obvious that he is motivated to find husbands for both his daughters not for their happiness, but to improve his own status and wealth. Anyone who will take Kate is welcome and, although he favors Bianca, he still wants to make a good bargain for her marriage. He ignores the happiness of both his daughters, and their own wishes are not of his concern.

THE SUITORS

Hortensio

These two characters play important roles in moving the action of the play. At the outset, Hortensio, a suitor of Bianca, shows his friendship for Petruchio by warning him about Kate. He dresses as a tutor to get close to Bianca, although it is quickly clear that she prefers Lucentio. When Hortensio becomes disenchanted with Bianca's behavior, he goes to Petruchio's taming school, where he hopes to learn how to keep the widow, whom he has decided to marry, in line. However, he does not learn to tame anything, and by play's end, it is clear that the widow will be the dominant partner in the marriage. Hortensio marries for money after ridiculing others for doing so.

Tranio

Tranio plays the lighthearted, quick-witted, and mischievous servant to Lucentio. He is loyal to the point that he poses as Lucentio to help him win Bianca and in fact acts much like a mentor or surrogate father, always offering advice on love and life. He is most amusing and clever when he hoodwinks the schoolteacher into posing as Lucentio's wealthy father.

CHRISTOPHER SLY

Although he appears only in the Induction and briefly at the end of the first scene in Act 1, Sly the tinker is a memorable character. He is a man who knows his place in the world, even when he is being tricked into thinking that place is somewhat higher than it actually is. He is loud and boastful, and his language is colorful. When he finally gives in and accepts that he is a lord, the audience senses that Sly has not really been fooled. Instead, he seems to be cooperating in the spirit of "let's enjoy this while it lasts."

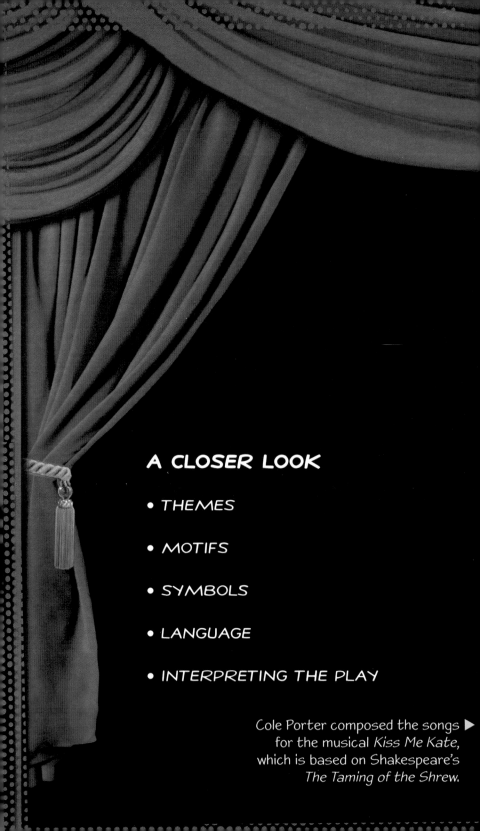

A CLOSER LOOK

- THEMES

- MOTIFS

- SYMBOLS

- LANGUAGE

- INTERPRETING THE PLAY

Cole Porter composed the songs ▶
for the musical *Kiss Me Kate*,
which is based on Shakespeare's
The Taming of the Shrew.

A Closer Look

THEMES

DISGUISE AND DECEIT

Many of Shakespeare's comedies, including this one, revolve around the use of disguise and deceit. With disguise the impossible becomes possible, and people become what they are not—at least for a time. Disguise is used to deceive others in order to bring about a desired end.

Three of the main characters in this comedy don disguises. Hortensio and Lucentio, who are from the upper class, both disguise themselves as tutors (Litio and Cambio, respectively). Both men want to win the hand of the lovely Bianca, and becoming her tutor seems the only way to get near her. With Lucentio disguised as Cambio, his servant Tranio takes on the garb of his master. Lucentio poses as Cambio until he marries Bianca.

Note that changing one's appearance in all three cases does not change the actual characters; they do not take on the personality traits of the person they are disguised as. Appearances, after all, can be deceiving.

The contrast of appearance and reality figures prominently in the characters of Kate and Petruchio. Kate is called a shrew—she is loud, rude, and cares little about others. By the end of the play, she is passive and seemingly in love with Petruchio. Has her personality really changed, or has she simply learned to act differently to have a happier life?

Even the lovely Bianca is not exactly what she seems. At the beginning of the play, she is portrayed as the dream of every Elizabethan male— fair, demure, and obedient. It is soon evident that she knows how to use these feminine wiles to get what she wants. She secretly defies her father by entertaining suitors and then elopes with one of them. After her marriage to Lucentio, she shows him that she is not as passive as she might have seemed. When Lucentio calls for her at the wedding feast, she refuses to appear.

There seems to be deception, too, in the character of Baptista, the father of Bianca and Kate. On the surface, he appears to be a caring, even doting parent. He provides his daughters with tutors in music and poetry, for instance, and speaks well of them. In the end, though, his precarious position wins out. His beautiful daughter Bianca, with the right marriage, can give him an increase in family fortune and status. With that end in mind, he is anxious to arrange a marriage for his older daughter, whatever her feelings. However, it must be remembered that most marriages among the upper class of the time were made based on monetary gain or a dowry.

In the Induction, Sly the tinker also uses deception at the same time that it is forced on him. At first unbelieving when he is told that he is in reality a lord—"do I dream?"—he quickly becomes convinced that he is indeed of the upper social class, if only to enjoy the benefits. "Upon my life, I am lord indeed," he says in Scene 2 of the Induction. Once again, Shakespeare reminds the audience that what is on the surface is often not reality.

THE BATTLE OF THE SEXES

The Taming of the Shrew is all about relationships between the sexes and their social roles. When it came to courting and marriage, the role of both women and men in Elizabethan England was strictly business. How the two people involved actually felt about each other was not considered too important. In the case of Baptista, a father's feelings for his daughters were not as important as the inheritance of money and an increase in the family fortune or social standing.

There has long been controversy about this comedy and its implied place of women in society. Early in the Induction, the lord gives instructions on how his male page, disguised as Sly's wife, should go about acting like a woman:

> WITH SOFT LOW TONGUE AND LOWLY COURTESY,
> AND SAY 'WHAT IS'T YOUR HONOUR WILL COMMAND,
> WHEREIN YOUR LADY AND YOUR HUMBLE WIFE
> MAY SHOW HER DUTY AND MAKE KNOWN HER LOVE?'

He is explaining the proper relationship between men and women, at least as men see it. From this perspective, it is easy to understand why Kate's rebelliousness upsets all the men around her.

Some critics say the mostly male audiences in Shakespeare's time would have delighted in the play. Others feel that many would have been turned off by the rough treatment of Kate. Petruchio never actually uses physical force in his attempt to subjugate Kate. In fact, in a sense the play is saying that as long as physical violence is not used, domination is acceptable.

As for modern audiences, the Welsh writer Stevie Davies in her book about this play, published in 1995, says that their reactions are "dominated by feelings of unease and embarrassment, accompanied by the desire to prove that Shakespeare cannot have meant what he seems to be saying; and that therefore he cannot really be saying it." It is often difficult to accept Elizabethan practices, such as treating women as property, because they are so different from the modern Western view.

John Fletcher, a writer in Shakespeare's time, was apparently bothered by the Bard's work. He wrote a kind of sequel called *The Woman's Prize, or the Tamer Tamed*. The date is uncertain, but it was probably published in the early part of the 1600s. In Fletcher's book, Kate has died; she was not tamed and her continued struggle with Petruchio was so harsh that it caused her death. Petruchio has remarried. His new wife, Maria, turns the tables and tames him.

Feminists in particular have attacked the play, particularly the last scene in which Kate seems to submit entirely and without question. Others say the play cannot be taken at face value. In the Induction, for instance, a drunken tinker could not be convinced that he is suddenly of royal birth. They say it is all just Shakespeare's way of playing with the social conventions that surrounded him.

Over the years, as the perception of the female role in society began to change, reactions to *The Taming of the Shrew* began to change as well. What was funny about the gradual and eventual domination of Kate by Petruchio began not to seem so amusing to many. In fact, in many instances even today the play is met by an unforgiving audience that is not afraid to shout disapproval at the actors on stage. The fact that reactions to the

"THIS IS A WAY TO KILL A WIFE WITH KINDNESS."

PETRUCHIO AND KATE ARE AT ODDS FOR MUCH OF THE PLAY BECAUSE THEY ARE SO ALIKE.

play are so varied and unpredictable probably accounts for its continued successful staging, especially among college and small theater groups.

CRUELTY

The longtime Shakespeare critic Marvin Krims has suggested cruelty as a theme for *The Taming of the Shrew*. There are other instances of what may be considered cruel behavior in addition to Petruchio's behavior in the taming of his wife. The cruelty may be emotional as well as physical.

In the Induction that begins the play, for example, the lord's treatment of Sly the tinker is emotionally cruel. The drunken tinker is encouraged to believe what deep down he knows is impossible. Petruchio's treatment of Kate on some levels can be considered emotionally cruel. He never physically abuses her, but he does withhold food and sleep. In addition, he is emotionally abusive by first claiming one thing and then immediately denying it when she agrees.

There are also numerous instances of physical cruelty in the play. In Act II, Scene 1, Kate has presumably bound Bianca's hands and strikes her when Bianca accuses Kate of being jealous of her suitors. Kate also hits Hortensio over the head with his lute: "I did but tell her she mistook her frets / . . . / And with that word she stroke me on the head, / And through the instrument my pate made way" (II.1).

Kate is not the only character who is physically violent. Grumio strikes fellow servant Curtis in Act IV, Scene 1, when Curtis asks to hear how Petruchio and Kate fell out of their saddles. The slap here is meant to be comical. Grumio explains that the story "'tis called a sensible tale, and this cuff was but to know at your ear and beseech list'ning." He makes a pun on "sensible," which means both rational and able to be physically felt. Later in the scene Petruchio strikes his servant who is pouring water. Kate intercedes, saying, "Patience, I pray you. 'Twas a fault unwilling." Petruchio also throws dishes at his servants when he is displeased (or pretending to be, at least) with the food. Again, Kate asks that he "be not so disquiet." Ironically, Kate is upset by Petruchio's ill-tempered and brash actions, despite the fact that he is only mimicking her own disposition.

MOTIFS

ANIMAL AND NATURE IMAGERY

Animal imagery is used throughout the play to help explain the characters. In the Induction, for instance, the lord says of the drunken tinker, "O monstrous beast! How like a swine he lies!" Kate, of course, is referred to as a shrew throughout the play. A shrew is a small, mouselike animal reported to be very feisty. Like an animal tamer, Petruchio is out to tame his shrewlike wife. In fact, when Hortensio visits him, Petruchio's home is referred to as a "taming school."

Petruchio uses animal imagery to discuss taming, or domesticating, Kate. He speaks of her as if she were his ox or horse. In Act III, Scene 2, he says,

> I WILL BE MASTER OF WHAT IS MINE OWN:
> SHE IS MY GOODS, MY CHATTELS; SHE IS MY HOUSE,
> MY HOUSEHOLD STUFF, MY FIELD, MY BARN,
> MY HORSE, MY OX, MY ASS, MY ANY THING.

In Act IV, Scene 1, Petruchio compares his treatment of Kate to that of a lord training a falcon:

> THUS HAVE I POLITICLY BEGUN MY REIGN,
> AND 'TIS MY HOPE TO END SUCCESSFULLY,
> MY FALCON NOW IS SHARP AND PASSING EMPTY;
> AND TILL SHE STOOP SHE MUST NOT BE FULL-GORGED.

In other words, Kate will not eat until she starts to behave in a better fashion. In Elizabethan England, the noblemen would train their hunting falcons with meat on a lure, or rope. If a falcon obeyed and chased the lure, the falconer would offer food as a reward. Similarly, Kate must obey Petruchio before he will give her something to eat.

There are many references to nature throughout the play. More than once, Petruchio identifies himself with the wind. In Act I, Scene 2, when he is newly arrived in Padua, he says he has been brought by the wind: "Such wind as scatters young men through the world / To seek their fortunes further than at home." Later, in Act II, Scene 1, he refers to himself as the wind that will blow out Kate's fire.

FATHERS AND CHILDREN

The differences in the way males and females were raised in Elizabethan times is another motif in the play. Men were expected to bring honor to the family name and to secure its fortunes. A male was educated because he in turn would preserve or enhance his family's lifestyle. Women were raised to marry, to add to her new family's fortunes with a dowry, and to bear children to carry on the family name. Wealth and social standing through marriage were highly prized among Elizabethan upper-class families.

There are three main father-child relationships: Vincentio and Lucentio, Baptista and Kate, and Baptista and Bianca. Note early in Act I, Scene I, that Lucentio has come to Padua for "A course of learning and ingenious studies." He speaks of his father as "A merchant of great traffic through the world." Therefore, Lucentio is bound "To deck his fortune with his virtuous deeds." Wealthy fathers of that time would have encouraged their sons to seek the best institutions of learning to bring both honor and fortune to the family.

Baptista's greatest concern is to marry off his older daughter, since, especially among the upper classes, it was customary—even necessary— for the firstborn female to marry first. In Act I, Scene 1, Baptista tells Gremio and Hortensio that they have his permission to court Kate. Baptista clearly prefers his younger child; in Act I, Scene 1, he wants to get her tutors: "And for I know she taketh most delight / In music, instruments and poetry, / Schoolmasters will I keep within my house, / Fit to instruct her youth." However, Baptista is also highly concerned with her marriage prospects. Her happiness matters far less to him than the social power and wealth a union might bring him. Bianca's education, in fact, will make her more appealing to a desirable suitor.

BIANCA KNOWS SHE IS HER
FATHER'S FAVORITE.

PETRUCHIO'S WEDDING ATTIRE

In Act III, Scene 2, Petruchio shows up at the church on his wedding day wearing a most disgraceful outfit. He is clad in old ripped clothing and rides a horse with a mothy saddle. Tranio feels there must be some purpose to this entrance: "He hath some meaning in his mad attire."

Baptista, who certainly is in favor of the marriage, is appalled at Petruchio's attire: "Why, sir, you know this is your wedding-day: / First we were sad, fearing you would not come; / Now sadder, that you come so unprovided, / Fie, doff this habit, shame to your estate." Baptista is thinking about reputation and wealth, and for him, Petruchio's attire is a symbol of his status. Petruchio offers no explanation for his appearance and asks where he can find Kate. Baptista knows his daughter will be even more outraged than he at Petruchio's get-up. "But thus, I trust, you will not marry her," he says to his soon-to-be son-in-law. Petruchio answers, "To me she's married, not unto my clothes," and sets off to find Kate. Baptista then follows Petruchio to see how Kate will react to his attire.

It may be true that Kate is not marrying his clothes, but Petruchio humiliates her by wearing such a ridiculous outfit. Thus, even before they are married, he is establishing control. If she refuses to marry Petruchio, she is disobeying her father's wishes and preventing Bianca from marrying Lucentio. If Kate goes through with the wedding and tolerates Petruchio's clownish outfit, only her pride suffers. She opts for the wedding to proceed, so Kate has lost authority at the very beginning of their marriage. However, Kate's choice also makes both her father and her sister happy.

KATE'S CAP AND GOWN

In Act IV, Scene 3, Kate's cap and gown are another symbol of Petruchio's hold over her. First, he speaks of the appearance of the tailor "To deck thy body with his ruffling treasure." The tailor arrives at Petruchio's home to make a cap and gown for Kate so that they can journey to her father's house in style. Kate finds the tailor's work appealing, and she is pleased. However, each time she expresses her pleasure, Petruchio denies it: "What's this? A sleeve? 'Tis like a demi-cannon." Petruchio is not happy with the result, or at least he says he is not, and sends the tailor away as Kate protests, "I never saw a better-fashioned gown." Even though there may be some depth to Petruchio's rejection because of his disdain for fine clothes, his authority is evident.

LANGUAGE

Shakespeare uses three forms of language in *The Taming of the Shrew*, as he does in all his plays: prose, rhymed verse, and blank verse. Prose is ordinary speech, unrhymed and unaccented, and not set as lines but as blocks of text. It is used for everyday conversation, as in Act IV, Scene 1, when Grumio speaks of Kate to Curtis at Petruchio's country home:

> SHE WAS, GOOD CURTIS, BEFORE THIS FROST; BUT, THOU KNOWEST, WINTER TAMES MAN, WOMAN AND BEAST; FOR IT HATH TAMED MY OLD MASTER AND MY NEW MISTRESS AND MYSELF, FELLOW CURTIS.

Rhymed verse usually has two adjacent lines that rhyme. As an example, in Act II, Scene 1, Baptista says to the servant Gremio:

> FAITH, GENTLEMEN, NOW I PLAY A MERCHANT'S PART, AND VENTURE MADLY ON A DESPERATE MART.

Blank verse, like prose, has no rhyme pattern. Most lines have ten syllables, alternating between stressed and unstressed. It has a regular rhythmic pattern when read aloud. The first word of each line is capitalized, and not all the lines are the same metric length. In Act IV, Scene 5, Kate says:

> YOUNG BUDDING VIRGIN, FAIR AND FRESH AND SWEET,
> WHITHER AWAY, OR WHERE IS THY ABODE?
> HAPPY THE PARENTS OF SO FAIR A CHILD;
> HAPPIER THE MAN, WHOM FAVOURABLE STARS
> ALLOT THEE FOR HIS LOVELY BED-FELLOW!

The use of language is highly important to the development of this play. Kate is characterized as a shrew largely because of her speech. She has a sharp tongue, is not loathe to use it, and cares little to whom she speaks. For example, in Act II, Scene 1, she says to Baptista:

> WHAT, WILL YOU NOT SUFFER ME? NAY, NOW I SEE
> SHE IS YOUR TREASURE, SHE MUST HAVE A HUSBAND;
> I MUST DANCE BARE-FOOT ON HER WEDDING DAY
> AND FOR YOUR LOVE TO HER LEAD APES IN HELL.

When she first meets Petruchio in the same act and scene, she says, "Asses are made to bear, and so are you," and when he names Sunday as their wedding day, she retorts, "I'll see thee hang'd on Sunday first."

Note also the subtle differences in the use of language among the characters in this play. When Sly is first introduced in the Induction, for instance, he uses language that is rough and vulgar as befits his station in society. When he begins to have aspirations of nobility, he becomes articulate and almost poetic. In fact, throughout the play, the characters of upper social status generally converse in verse, whereas those of a lower station do so in prose.

Also pertinent to the language of the play is the evident snobbery of the upper class. In Act III, Scene 1, Hortensio begins to suspect that Bianca actually cares for Lucentio, who is in disguise as a tutor. Hortensio says, "If once I find thee ranging," meaning if she really does care for someone of a lower social status, he will immediately leave her alone and find someone else. In this scene, Hortensio himself is playing a person of lower social standing—a tutor—but he reveals his true self when he speaks.

Much has been made of Kate's final speech in the play. She seems to accept fully her new role as a submissive, obedient wife. But has she? There are two schools of thought among the critics. Some say she is sincere. She rationalizes the social and political submission of wives to husbands. Therefore, she has been successfully tamed. Others contend that Kate is not sincere at all; she is actually being sarcastic and mocking the entire concept of female submission. The interpretation of this speech will affect the entire tone of the play. In fact, the way a director interprets the meaning of this final speech often defines the tone of the production. Only Shakespeare knew for sure.

INTERPRETING THE PLAY

HISTORICAL CONTENT

Through the years, Shakespeare's authorship of *The Taming of the Shrew* has been questioned because another work with a similar title, *The Taming of a Shrew*, was published about the same time. It is said to have different characters but a similar plot. The authorship is unknown, although some have said that Shakespeare wrote both. Others disagree.

Although this play may seem chauvinistic to modern audiences, it must be considered in its historical context. In Shakespeare's day, legal and moral rights of women, how they should behave, and what they should wear were matters that were differently understood than they are today. In marriage, the traditional view of the husband as the family's ultimate authority figure was the societal norm.

A ballad composed around 1550 entitled *A Merry Jest of a Shrewd and Curst Wife Lapped in Morel's Skin, for Her Good Behavior* spoke of proper treatment for uncooperative women in Elizabethan England. It was printed only once, but Shakespeare likely would have known of it or seen it. In this ballad, as in *The Taming of the Shrew*, there are two sisters; one is shrewish, the other is favored by the father. The shrewish daughter marries a man who decides to change her ways by beating her and wrapping her in salted horsehide. Not unexpectedly, the woman becomes docile and obedient. It was quite popular with Elizabethans.

INFLUENCES OF *THE TAMING OF THE SHREW*

This farce from Shakespeare has remained a favorite on stage and screen and in television adaptations despite the fact that some consider it blatantly sexist. Not all stagings of the play, however, have met with success. Some audiences have reacted with hostility to the treatment of Kate; some have loudly booed and even thrown things at the actors.

The earliest known performance was on June 13, 1594; it is recorded in Elizabethan theatrical entrepreneur Philip Henslowe's diary as "the Tamynge of A Shrowe." Some scholars assume that the play in question was Shakespeare's play rather than a similar play or an adaptation, but there is much disagreement in this matter. The Shakespeare version is known to have been performed in 1633, when King Charles I was in the audience.

In 1935 a now-famous production of the play was staged by New York's Theatre Guild. The production starred Alfred Lunt and Lynn Fontanne and ran for 129 performances.

On December 30, 1948, the first of many theater audiences became enchanted with a new musical comedy on Broadway in New York City. It featured the music of the famed songwriter Cole Porter as well as the talents of two great stage actors, Alfred Drake and Patricia Morison. The show ran for 1,077 performances—a hit in any year. Many in the audiences would have been surprised to know they were watching a play based loosely on *The Taming of the Shrew*. The musical was *Kiss Me, Kate*.

In this modernized plot, two recently divorced actors are starring together in a musical version of the Shakespeare work. On opening night, Lilli gets a bouquet of flowers that she assumes are from her ex-husband, Fred. Before the curtain goes up, however, she finds out that the flowers were intended for another woman. The stage now becomes a battlefield. In the end, they realize they truly love one another.

The musical, which has since been revived many times, won Tony awards for best musical, score and librettist, producer, and costume design. Most critics and audiences felt as did one journalist who wrote, "Kiss me, Kate, again, again, and again."

Hollywood became enchanted as well. D. W. Griffith produced a silent version of this Shakespeare comedy in 1908. The first "talkie" version starred the film industry's darlings Mary Pickford and Douglas Fairbanks in 1929. In 1950 the Westinghouse Studio/CBS film starred Lisa Kirk and Charlton Heston. In 1953 Howard Keel and Kathryn Grayson starred in a successful version, but probably the best-remembered production was released in 1967. It showcased two of the silver screen's most talked-about stars, Elizabeth Taylor and Richard Burton, who were married at the time. With one million dollars of their own money invested in the film, the result was a great success and received two Oscar nominations.

Television got involved with *The Taming of the Shrew* as early as 1952 with a BBC production. In 1980, Jonathan Miller produced a praised adaptation for BBC/Time-Life Television. It starred Sarah Badel and John Cleese. The BBC's *ShakespeaRe-Told* series transferred the story to present-day Britain, where Kate is a career politician who is told to find a husband if she wants to improve her image. In the end, she still gives a speech on a woman's duty to love and obey her husband; only this time, he is required to do the same.

In 2000 a Brazilian soap opera, *O Cravo e a Rosa* (The Carnation and the Rose), was based on Shakespeare's farce. The title comes from a children's song that talks about a couple of flowers that had a serious "fight."

TONE

In a play, tone refers to *how* things are said and done. Tone is expressed in the play's many parts—the language, symbols, images, and diction that form the action. The tone of *The Taming of the Shrew* is above all playful and light. The play may be—and is—often criticized for its perhaps too playful or too light handling of "woman taming." However, the overall action and speech of the characters, including the opening joke played on Sly the tinker, are always light and bantering rather than heavy-handed. Although it is a farce, the exploration of larger social questions, such as the role of the sexes in marriage, lends an underlying serious quality to the play.

The reader or viewer may find the joke on Sly or the handling of Kate offensive in some regard, but it is difficult not to laugh at the quick-witted banter that drives the action of the play. It is easy to believe that Shakespeare was laughing at the customs and conventions of the time, even if he might have approved of them. Through the lighthearted way in which the action proceeds, the audience gets a good glimpse of life in Elizabethan times, with its time-honored beliefs and mores that often seem strange to modern viewers.

Chronology

1564 William Shakespeare is born on April 23 in Stratford-upon-Avon, England

1578-1582 Span of Shakespeare's "Lost Years," covering the time between leaving school and marrying Anne Hathaway of Stratford

1582 At age eighteen Shakespeare marries Anne Hathaway, age twenty-six, on November 28

1583 Susanna Shakespeare, William and Anne's first child, is born in May, six months after the wedding

1584 Birth of twins Hamnet and Judith Shakespeare

1585-1592 Shakespeare leaves his family in Stratford to become an actor and playwright in a London theater company

1587 Public beheading of Mary, Queen of Scots

1593-1594 The Bubonic (Black) Plague closes theaters in London

1594-1596 As a leading playwright, Shakespeare creates some of his most popular work, including *A Midsummer Night's Dream* and *Romeo and Juliet*

1596 Hamnet Shakespeare dies in August at age eleven, possibly of plague

1596–1597	*The Merchant of Venice* and *Henry IV, Part One,* most likely are written
1599	The Globe Theater opens
1600	*Julius Caesar* is first performed at the Globe
1600–1601	*Hamlet* is believed to have been written
1601–1602	*Twelfth Night* is probably composed
1603	Queen Elizabeth dies; Scottish king James VI succeeds her and becomes England's James I
1604	Shakespeare pens *Othello*
1605	*Macbeth* is composed
1608–1610	London's theaters are forced to close when the plague returns and kills an estimated 33,000 people
1611	*The Tempest* is written
1613	The Globe Theater is destroyed by fire
1614	Reopening of the Globe
1616	Shakespeare dies on April 23
1623	Anne Hathaway, Shakespeare's widow, dies; a collection of Shakespeare's plays, known as the First Folio, is published

Source Notes

p. 41, par. 4, For a look at the differences between wedding customs in Elizabethan England and modern times, *see* www.william-shakespeare.info/elizabethan-wedding-customs.htm.

p. 44, par. 3, Take a virtual tour of Padua, one of Italy's loveliest cities, where so much of the action of *The Taming of the Shrew* takes place. *See* www.virtourist.com/europe/padua/Padua_Italy.htm.

p. 49, par. 2, Most of the upper classes in Elizabethan times had servants, and most of the servants in any household were men. Serving men were generally referred to as grooms; serving women were maids or serving maids. Ladies-in-waiting served only the queen. Both servant and master worked to the credit of each other. It was beneath a lady's dignity to carry her own shopping basket, for instance; nor would her maid want her to. A gentleman would expect that his personal servant would be well dressed and act accordingly. As in many occupations, a clever servant expected to rise in the household. A groom in the stable might aspire to become a butler. A seamstress might look for a chance to become the favored maid of the lady of the house.

p. 68, par. 2, Petruchio speaks of taming Kate much as he would tame a falcon. Beginning in the Middle Ages, falconry was an important part of life in England. In fact, falcons were the first birds to be protected by law. The first known falconer was Ethelbert II, the Saxon king of Kent. Falconry was restricted to the upper classes. Only the king and nobility could have noble, long-winged falcons such as peregrines and merlins. In addition to being hunting birds, falcons were also symbols of power and strength. They were frequently found on banners and coats of arms.

The falconer's position was handed down from father to son. The Lord Falconer in a royal household captured, trained, and cared for these powerful birds. He occupied the fourth position from the king at the dining table. He also went to war with the king and brought the birds along for the hunt. For instance, when Edward III invaded France (1339–1340), thirty falconers went with him. Henry VIII (reigned 1509–1547) was a great admirer of the sport, as was Mary Queen of Scots and her cousin, Elizabeth I. Mary became Elizabeth's prisoner in 1568 (she was wanted for the murder of her husband in Scotland) at Bolton Castle. Mary's imprisonment was one of luxury. On occasion, Elizabeth even allowed her outside on the castle grounds for falcon hunts—under supervision, of course.

Falconry was an expensive pursuit. The birds required a specialized diet and housing. As forests were transformed into farmland, falconry largely faded into memory.

p. 68, par. 5, The meals of the upper class during Shakespeare's time differed considerably from those of lower social standing. For one thing, the upper classes did not eat many vegetables; in fact, the word *vegetable* was rarely used among them. Food that came from the ground was considered more fitting for the lower classes. Ironically, therefore, the poorer in England usually ate a healthier diet!

The upper class ate from silverware; lower classes used wooden dishes. They used knives but rarely spoons, as most liquid, even soup, was drunk from a cup. There were many meat dishes, such as venison, beef, and pork. Only lords and other nobles were allowed to hunt deer or rabbits; the penalty for poaching was having one's hands cut off. The upper class enjoyed a wide variety of fish and various spices imported from abroad.

Breakfast was generally served between six and seven each morning. Dinner was eaten between twelve and two. Supper, usually a heavy meal, was served between six and seven and often included entertainment.

p. 74, par. 1, This is the wedding day of Lucentio and Bianca. Although Bianca's age is not stated, in that day and age it was legal for girls to marry at the age of twelve and legal for boys at fourteen. Weddings generally took place at the local church and were conducted by a minister. The first step in a marriage, a custom still carried out in England today, is called Crying the Banns, and it takes place before the ceremony. As per custom, the intention to marry was supposed to be announced three times before the actual ceremony. There is no mention of this custom in Shakespeare's play.

There were no wedding invitations, but gifts were accepted. As today, family and friends attended. The bride might wear whatever color she chose, as white did not become the accepted bridal color until much later. After the ceremony, the wedding procession moved to the bride's home, where there was food and entertainment in the form of musicians. Afterward, everyone went home.

A Shakespeare Glossary

The student should not try to memorize these, but only refer to them as needed. We can never stress enough that the best way to learn Shakespeare's language is simply to *hear* it—to hear it spoken well by good actors. After all, small children master every language on Earth through their ears, without studying dictionaries, and we should master Shakespeare, as much as possible, the same way.

addition — a name or title (knight, duke, duchess, king, etc.)
admire — to marvel
affect — to like or love; to be attracted to
an — if ("An I tell you that, I'll be hanged.")
approve — to prove or confirm
attend — to pay attention
belike — probably
beseech — to beg or request
betimes — soon; early
bondman — a slave
bootless — futile; useless; in vain
broil — a battle
charge — expense, responsibility; to command or accuse
clepe, clept — to name; named
common — of the common people; below the nobility
conceit — imagination
condition — social rank; quality
countenance — face; appearance; favor
cousin — a relative
cry you mercy — beg your pardon
curious — careful; attentive to detail
dear — expensive
discourse — to converse; conversation
discover — to reveal or uncover
dispatch — to speed or hurry; to send; to kill
doubt — to suspect

entreat — to beg or appeal

envy — to hate or resent; hatred; resentment

ere — before

ever, e'er — always

eyne — eyes

fain — gladly

fare — to eat; to prosper

favor — face, privilege

fellow — a peer or equal

filial — of a child toward his or her parent

fine — an end; "in fine" = in sum

fond — foolish

fool — a darling

genius — a good or evil spirit

gentle — well-bred; not common

gentleman — one whose labor was done by servants (Note: to call someone a *gentleman* was not a mere compliment on his manners; it meant that he was above the common people.)

gentles — people of quality

get — to beget (a child)

go to — "go on"; "come off it"

go we — let us go

haply — perhaps

happily — by chance; fortunately

hard by — nearby

heavy — sad or serious

husbandry — thrift; economy

instant — immediate

kind — one's nature; species

knave — a villain; a poor man

lady — a woman of high social rank (Note: *lady* was not a synonym for *woman* or *polite woman*; it was not a compliment, but, like *gentleman*, simply a word referring to one's actual legal status in society.)

leave — permission; "take my leave" = depart (with permission)

lief, lieve — "I had as lief" = I would just as soon; I would rather

like — to please; "it likes me not" = it is disagreeable to me

livery — the uniform of a nobleman's servants; emblem
mark — notice; pay attention
morrow — morning
needs — necessarily
nice — too fussy or fastidious
owe — to own
passing — very
peculiar — individual; exclusive
privy — private; secret
proper — handsome; one's very own ("his proper son")
protest — to insist or declare
quite — completely
require — request
several — different; various
severally — separately
sirrah — a term used to address social inferiors
sooth — truth
state — condition; social rank
still — always; persistently
success — result(s)
surfeit — fullness
touching — concerning; about; as for
translate — to transform
unfold — to disclose
villain — a low or evil person; originally, a peasant
voice — a vote; consent; approval
vouchsafe — to confide or grant
vulgar — common
want — to lack
weeds — clothing
what ho — "hello, there!"
wherefore — why
wit — intelligence; sanity
withal — moreover; nevertheless
without — outside
would — wish

Suggested Essay Topics

1. Today, the idea that a wife should be subservient to her husband is not widely held. Outline Elizabethan attitudes on this subject, and discuss whether they contributed to making *The Taming of the Shrew* popular in its own day.

2. *The Taming of the Shrew* is a farce. What are some characteristics of a farce? Do you think Petruchio really loves Kate by the end of the play? Explain your answer. Do you think Kate really falls in love with Petruchio? Explain.

3. Was Baptista a loving father? How did his treatment of his two daughters differ? Why? Give instances throughout the play that indicate changes in Kate's personality.

Testing Your Memory

1. Sly the tinker first appears in what part of the play? a) Prologue;
   b) Induction; c) Act I, Scene 1; d) Epilogue

2. In what city does most of the play take place? a) London; b) Verona;
   c) Venice; d) Padua

3. Why does Lucentio disguise himself as a tutor? a) He has fallen for
   Bianca and wants to be close to her; b) His father wants him to be a
   teacher; c) He needs the money; d) He promised his father he would
   work while in Padua.

4. What does Kate do soon after she meets Petruchio? a) She falls in love;
   b) She hits him; c) She cries; d) She laughs at him.

5. Why is Baptista so concerned with finding a husband for Kate?
   a) He needs the money; b) He does not love her; c) He fears she is
   too ugly to marry; d) In Shakespeare's time, the eldest daughter was
   expected to marry first.

6. Tranio disguises himself as what character? a) Hortensio; b) Vincentio;
   c) Lucentio; d) Gremio

7. The main action of the play, the relationship between Petruchio and
   Kate, is an example of what genre? a) melodrama; b) farce;
   c) nonfiction; d) satire

8. What does Kate ask Grumio to do at Petruchio's home? a) get a horse so
   she can escape; b) get her new clothes; c) write a letter to her father; d)
   bring her food

9. How did most Elizabethans regard a woman's role in marriage?
   a) She should be an equal partner; b) She should be a good cook;
   c) She should be loving and obedient; d) She should never cry.

10. When Vincentio arrives in Padua and no one recognizes him, what does he think has happened to his son Lucentio? a) He thinks Lucentio has been murdered; b) He thinks Lucentio has married; c) He thinks Lucentio has returned to Florence; d) He has no opinion.

11. Before entering Lucentio's wedding feast, what does Petruchio ask Kate to do? a) kiss him in public; b) change her clothes; c) dance with him; d) make him laugh

12. What does Kate do at the wedding celebration that causes trouble? a) She dances with Lucentio; b) She nearly has a fight with the widow; c) She nearly has a fight with Petruchio; d) She nearly has a fight with Bianca.

13. How does Petruchio arrive at the church for his wedding? a) in a tuxedo; b) in a robe; c) in mismatched clothes; d) in his underwear

14. Where do Petruchio and Kate go after their wedding? a) to his country home; b) to the wedding feast; c) to Baptista's home; d) on a honeymoon

15. When Lucentio calls for Bianca at the wedding feast, how does she reply? a) She says that she will come immediately; b) She says she is too busy to come; c) She demands that he come to her; d) She refuses to answer.

16. When Hortensio calls for the widow at the wedding feast, how does she reply? a) She demands that he come to her; b) She says she is too busy; c) She says she will come right away; d) She refuses to answer.

17. When Petruchio calls for Kate at the wedding feast, what does she do? a) She appears immediately; b) She refuses to come; c) She says she is too busy; d) She demands that he come to her.

Answer Key

Further Information

Books

The Taming of the Shrew. Folger Shakespeare Library. Edited by Barbara A. Mowat and Paul Werstine. New York: Simon & Schuster, 2004.

The Taming of the Shrew. The New Cambridge Shakespeare. Edited by Ann Thompson. New York: Cambridge University Press, 2003.

The Taming of the Shrew. The Oxford Shakespeare. Edited by H. J. Oliver. New York: Oxford University Press, 2008.

Websites

http://absoluteshakespeare.com
Absolute Shakespeare is a resource for the Bard's plays, sonnets, and poems and includes summaries, quotes, films, trivia, and more.

www.playshakespeare.com
Play Shakespeare features all the play texts with an online glossary, reviews, a discussion forum, and links to festivals worldwide.

www.william-shakespeare.info/shakespeare-play-the-taming-of-the-shrew.htm
William Shakespeare: The Complete Works provides links related to the specific plays, as well as articles about Shakespeare's life, world, and works.

Bibliography

William Shakespeare

Clark, William George, and William Aldis Wright. *The Complete Works of William Shakespeare.* New York: Grosset, 1911.

Fallon, Robert Thomas. *A Theatergoer's Guide to Shakespeare.* Chicago: Dee, 2001.

The Taming of the Shrew

Marvel, Laura, ed. *Readings on "The Taming of the Shrew."* San Diego, CA: Greenhaven, 2000.

Index

Page numbers in **boldface** are illustrations.

Index

Page numbers in **boldface** are illustrations.

About the Author

A former children's book editor and U.S. Navy journalist, Corinne J. Naden has written more than ninety books for children and young adults, including *Romeo and Juliet* and *As You Like It* in this series. She lives in Tarrytown, New York.